Sustainable Development Goal 3

T0316360

Sustainable Development Goals (SDGs) aim to develop a better and sustainable future for the world, and the goals are part of an action plan to address poverty, hunger, health, gender equity and various pressing world issues. One of these goals looks at health and wellness. Ageing populations have become a crucial issue worldwide, and this short monograph explores ageing and how the consequences of an ageing population may affect our healthcare system through a case study on Hong Kong's population.

The book looks at several critical health issues related to ageing. The elderly, particularly those with low socio-economic status, rely more on acute-centric care rather than primary care. The book suggests that secondary care service may only be effective to a limited extent as a healthcare measure and an optimum healthcare system should be one that focuses on primary care. The authors put forth a compelling argument for disease prevention and screening schemes and explain how they are more cost-effective and beneficial to society and the system.

This thoughtful book will provide beneficial insights into the relationship of ageing and Sustainable Development Goals in the context of health and wellness for policymakers and healthcare professionals.

Ben Y. F. Fong is Associate Division Head of the Division of Science, Engineering and Health Studies of the College of Professional and Continuing Education, and is Centre Director of the Centre for Ageing and Healthcare Management Research of the School of Professional Education and Executive Development of The Hong Kong Polytechnic University (PolyU SPEED), Hong Kong, China.

Vincent T. S. Law is a Senior Lecturer at the School of Professional Education and Executive Development of The Hong Kong Polytechnic University (PolyU SPEED).

Routledge Focus on Public Governance in Asia

Series Editors: Hong Liu
Nanyang Technological University, Singapore

Wenxuan Yu
Xiamen University, China

Focusing on new governance challenges, practices and experiences in and about a globalizing Asia, particularly East Asia and Southeast Asia, this focus series invites upcoming and established researchers all over the world to succinctly and comprehensively discuss important public administration and policy themes such as government administrative reform, public budgeting reform, government crisis management, public – private partnership, science and technology policy, technology-enabled public service delivery, public health and aging, talent management, and anti-corruption across Asian countries. The book series presents compact and concise content under 50,000 words long which has significant theoretical contributions to the governance theory with an Asian perspective and practical implications for administration and policy reform and innovation.

Collaborative Governance of Local Governments in China
Jing Cui

Local Government Innovativeness in China
Youlang Zhang

Talent Strategies and Leadership Development of the Public Sector
Insights from Southeast Asia
Celia Lee

Sustainable Development Goal 3
Health and Well-being of Ageing in Hong Kong
Ben Y. F. Fong and Vincent T. S. Law

For more information about this series, please visit www.routledge.com/ Routledge-Focus-on-Public-Governance-in-Asia/book-series/RFPGA

Sustainable Development Goal 3

Health and Well-being of Ageing in Hong Kong

Ben Y. F. Fong and Vincent T. S. Law

*With contributions from Tiffany C. H. Leung,
Man Fung Lo, Tommy K. C. Ng and Hilary H. L. Yee*

Routledge
Taylor & Francis Group

LONDON AND NEW YORK

First published 2022
by Routledge
4 Park Square, Milton Park, Abingdon, Oxon OX14 4RN

and by Routledge
605 Third Avenue, New York, NY 10158

Routledge is an imprint of the Taylor & Francis Group, an informa business

British Library Cataloguing-in-Publication Data
A catalogue record for this book is available from the British Library

Library of Congress Cataloging-in-Publication Data
Names: Fong, Ben Y. F., author.
Title: Sustainable development goal 3: health and well-being of ageing in Hong Kong / Ben Y. F. Fong, [and five others].
Other titles: Sustainable development goal three
Description: Milton Park, Abingdon, Oxon ; New York, NY : Routledge, 2022. | Series: Focus on public governance in Asia | Includes bibliographical references and index.
Identifiers: LCCN 2021043919 (print) | LCCN 2021043920 (ebook)
Subjects: LCSH: Sustainable development—China—Hong Kong. | Economic development—Government policy—China—Hong Kong. | Population aging—China—Hong Kong.
Classification: LCC HC470.3.Z9 E5 2022 (print) | LCC HC470.3.Z9 (ebook) | DDC 338.95125—dc23
LC record available at https://lccn.loc.gov/2021043919
LC ebook record available at https://lccn.loc.gov/2021043920

ISBN: 978-1-032-11509-2 (hbk)
ISBN: 978-1-032-11501-6 (pbk)
ISBN: 978-1-003-22016-9 (ebk)

DOI: 10.4324/9781003220169

Typeset in Times New Roman
by Apex CoVantage, LLC

Contents

Foreword

It gives me great pleasure to write the Foreword for this book, *Sustainable Development Goal 3: Health and Well-being of Ageing in Hong Kong*, written by colleagues of the Centre for Ageing and Healthcare Management Research of our university.

Given the pervasive and rapid ageing situation around the world, the United Nations' Sustainable Development Goal 3 (SDG 3) – "ensure healthy lives and promote well-being for all at all ages" – is not likely to be attained unless there is a concerted effort from different academic disciplines to come up with practical and cost-effective solutions for governments and other stakeholders.

The authors of this book are experienced academics and professionals in the field of medicine, public policy, social and environmental accounting, and knowledge management. It analyses the interconnection of various SDGs to ageing using Hong Kong as a case study. It seeks to devise solutions that contributes to the well-being of the elderly population focusing on the sustainability of the health and long-term care system. I am confident that this publication will benefit healthcare practitioners, policymakers, academics and students.

Peter P. Yuen
Dean, College of Professional and Continuing Education
Professor, Department of Management and Marketing
Advisor, Centre for Ageing and Healthcare Management Research
School of Professional Education and Executive Development
The Hong Kong Polytechnic University

Acknowledgements

The authors and co-authors wish to thank Professor Peter P. Yuen for writing the foreword and Lit Kam Kong and Lam Ting Yu, Student Research Assistants of the Centre for Ageing and Healthcare Management Research (CAHMR) at the School of Professional Education and Executive Development of The Hong Kong Polytechnic University, for their academic input and contributions. The work described in this book was fully supported by a grant from the Research Grants Council of the Hong Kong Special Administrative Region, China (Project Reference No.: UGC/IDS24/18). In addition, the continuing support and expert advice from Yongling Lam and her team at Routledge have expedited the publication. We are also appreciative and grateful to our readers who are dedicated to the health and well-being of the elderly and to the realisation of the sustainability development goals established by the United Nations.

Authors and co-authors

Authors

Ben Y. F. Fong is Specialist in Community Medicine, holding Honorary Clinical Associate Professorship at the two local medical schools in Hong Kong, China. He is currently Professor of Practice (Health Studies) and Associate Division Head of the Division of Science, Engineering and Health Studies of the College of Professional and Continuing Education, and is Centre Director of the Centre for Ageing and Healthcare Management Research of the School of Professional Education and Executive Development of The Hong Kong Polytechnic University (PolyU). He has contributed to publications, including *The Routledge Handbook of Public Health and the Community* (as Lead Editor, 2021), *Primary Care Revisited: Interdisciplinary Perspectives for a New Era* (as Lead Editor, 2020), a training manual for general practitioners in China published by the People's Medical Publishing House in Beijing (as Co-editor, published in 2020), over 30 health books in Chinese, and 60 journal papers.

Vincent T. S. Law is Senior Lecturer of the School of Professional Education and Executive Development (SPEED) of The Hong Kong Polytechnic University (PolyU). Vincent is also Founding Member and Academic Convenor of the Centre for Ageing and Healthcare Management Research (CAHMR) of PolyU SPEED. Being an experienced researcher in public policy, Vincent participated in some large-scale consultancy or research projects on public policy and public engagement with the Hong Kong government in recent years. He authored a few academic journal papers and book chapters on health care and sustainability, and published four Chinese books on Chinese wisdom.

Co-authors

Tiffany C. H. Leung is Assistant Professor in the Faulty of Business at the City University of Macau. She is Founding Member of the Centre for

Ageing and Healthcare Management Research (CAHMR) of the School of Professional Education and Executive Development (SPEED) at The Hong Kong Polytechnic University. She is also Coordinator in the Centre for Social and Environmental Accounting Research (CSEAR) North Asia Office in Hong Kong and Macau. Besides, she serves as Editorial Board of *Social and Environmental Accountability Journal*, Board Member of *Accounting Forum* and Ad Hoc Reviewers in a number of management and accounting journals. She has also published peer-reviewed articles in management, business ethics and sustainability accounting journals.

Man Fung Lo is Lecturer of the Faculty of Social Science, The Chinese University of Hong Kong. Man Fung is also Founding Member of the Centre for Ageing and Healthcare Management Research (CAHMR) of the School of Professional Education and Executive Development, The Hong Kong Polytechnic University (PolyU SPEED). In addition, he is accredited as Senior Practitioner (FEDIPSnrPra) of The Federation for Informatics Professions in Health and Social Care, UK. His research areas are knowledge management and information technology, and his work has been published in academic journals, such as *Journal of Knowledge Management*, *Leadership & Organization Development Journal*, *Higher Education Quarterly* and *Asia Pacific Journal of Management*.

Tommy K. C. Ng is Project Associate in the Centre for Ageing and Healthcare Management Research (CAHMR) of the School of Professional Education and Executive Development (SPEED) at The Hong Kong Polytechnic University. In this position at CAHMR, he is actively involved in research related to health topics and is responsible for organising different research activities, including conferences, research seminars and methodology workshops. He has published several journal papers in various topics and a book chapter in primary care.

Hilary H. L. Yee is Research Assistant in the Centre for Ageing and Healthcare Management Research (CAHMR) of the School of Professional Education and Executive Development (SPEED) at The Hong Kong Polytechnic University. She has participated in several journal papers in various topics, including palliative care, elderly home safety, lifelong education and service learning for the elderly.

1 Global impacts of the Sustainable Development Goals

The United Nations (UN) is showing supremely aspirational and transformational visions to resolve unpleasant life events that threaten human beings through the development of 17 Sustainable Development Goals (SDGs) with 169 targets in 2015 (United Nations, 2021a). The Division for Sustainable Development Goals (DSDG) in the United Nations Department of Economic and Social Affairs (UNDESA) aims to offer substantive support and capacity-building for all the SDGs with its purposes and principles that are fully compatible with international laws, with respect to issues concerning water, energy, climate, oceans, urbanisation, transport, science and technology. The ambition of the SDGs is to apply to all nations, particularly the developing countries, in creating a new worldview that may help them to mobilise collective actions and share information with the developed countries. All 17 SDGs are adopted by all member states of the UN with the objectives to end poverty and hunger, to achieve equalities within and among countries, to build peaceful societies, to protect human rights and to protect the lasting natural resources from climate change. To achieve the SDGs, policy changes and political work will certainly require entrepreneurial actions at this stage. The policymakers have to focus more on the collaboration efforts between developing and developed countries. Although progress on achieving the SDGs by 2030 is much being disrupted by the COVID-19 pandemic, different countries are making some ongoing progress towards different SDGs. An overview of the 17 SDGs and the achievements with multi-targets that pursue global development and international collaboration in developing and developed countries are described for each SDG with case examples from different parts of the world.

Goal 1: end poverty in all its forms everywhere

SDG 1 is set up to end all the poverty, improve social protection and ensure the poor and the vulnerable have equal access to economic resources by

DOI: 10.4324/9781003220169-1

2030. It also targets building the resilience of the poor and vulnerable, and reducing the exposure to negative consequences caused by extreme events or environmental disasters. Creating sound social protection policy frameworks from the international levels, it supports increased investment in eradicating poverty.

Ending extreme poverty should be prioritised as one in ten people still suffer from acute poverty every day (Dhahri & Omri, 2020). The savings-based microfinance programme carried out by Cooperative for Assistance and Relief Everywhere, better and widely known as CARE International and founded in 1945, in various parts of Zimbabwe have helped people to improve household livelihoods by acquiring physical farming assets, such as wheelbarrows, ploughs and hoes (Kabonga et al., 2021). Among the emerging economies, India has the largest reduction in extreme poverty. The Government of India has implemented multipronged welfare scheme in areas of health, education, housing, skills development and social protection, resulting in increased pension and health insurance coverage, and decreased proportion of homeless people and poverty gap ration between rural and urban areas (Ministry of Statistics and Programme Implementation, 2021). Whereas in China and Mexico, the rural minimum living standard guarantee (Dibao) programme and conditional cash transfer programme have benefited 75 and 32 million individuals, respectively (Hanna & Olken, 2018). China announced in 2021 the eradication of poverty, which has been regarded as a very special experience involving massive mobilisation of resources while not affecting the already fast development in other parts of the vast country at the same time. It is suggested to study the Chinese experience around the world, particularly the poor nations (Global Times, 2021).

Goal 2: end hunger, achieve food security and improved nutrition, and promote sustainable agriculture

SDG 2 desires to end hunger and achieve food security by all people, in particular the poor and vulnerable people, by 2030. It is also promoting agricultural productivity, including resources and inputs, knowledge of financial services, and opportunities for small-scale food producers. These strategies can help to promote genetic diversity of seeds, cultivated plants and domestic animals, thus ensuring sustainable food production systems. To encourage and increase productivity in developing countries, technology development in agricultural research is also targeted.

African countries are unlikely to achieve the SDG 2 "Zero Hunger" by 2030. The food insecurity experience scale had measured a moderate to severe food insecurity from 2014 to 2019, and the estimated rate of undernourishment would be increased from 19.1% to 25.7% by 2030 (Atukunda et al., 2021). Therefore, African governments are collaborating with several specialised UN agencies to carry out programmes to end hunger. For instance, the Monitoring and Analysing Food and Agricultural Policies (MAFAP) provides evidence to support informed policy dialogue at the national, regional and international levels that helps to understand how different food and agricultural policies work in various contexts across the 14 Sub-Saharan African countries (Pernechele et al., 2018). The Food and Agriculture Organisation of the UN provides education to communities on good farming practices to increase incomes. Another example is changing the social norms and preventing excluding women from resource ownership and farming services in the UN Development Programme. Such collective commitment involving different stakeholders is important in helping African countries to strive for zero hunger in the long term (Pernechele et al., 2018).

Pertinently, a good agroforestry system ensures a sustainable food production system and helps to maintain well-established agricultural practices to sustain SDG 2 in both developing and developed countries (Montagnini & Metzel, 2017). The project "Tree Crops Development in Africa and Asia to Benefit the Poor", active in Cameroon, Ghana, Kenya, Mali and India, helps smallholder farming systems of fruits, nuts and oil seed trees to transit into semicommercial farming and large-scale commercial enterprises (Montagnini & Metzel, 2017). It involves research and development on soil conservation, genetic diversity and cultivation strategies for target tree plantation and related products. Thus, research can assist to identify the priorities of species most useful for alleviating food insecurity in each target region.

Goal 3: ensure healthy lives and promote well-being for all at all ages

SDG 3 aims at seeking more comprehensive healthy lives for all along each stage of life. The first target is to reduce the global maternal mortality ratio below 70 per 1 million live births and prevent deaths of newborns to 12 per 1,000 live births. Governments have to pay more attention to strengthen the foundation of healthy lives by achieving universal health coverage, prevention of substance abuse, and access to sexual and reproductive healthcare services. Furthermore, epidemics of AIDS, tuberculosis, malaria and neglected tropical diseases should be ended, and research on vaccines and medicines for infectious diseases and non-communicable diseases (NCD) should be supported (UN, 2021b).

In the study by Fullman et al. (2017), they measured 37 health-related indicators worldwide, and gains and gaps for health-related performances varied across 188 developed and developing countries. The results showed that globally, 60% of countries were projected to achieve reduction in maternal mortality ratio, neonatal mortality and malaria, but only 6% and 3% of countries were projected to reduce mortality of NCD and suicide rate, respectively, by 2030 (Fullman et al., 2017). Issues of HIV, tuberculosis, childhood overweight and mortality of road injury are yet to demonstrate progressive achievement, as less than 7% of countries were projected to meet the SDG targets. The best performers of health-related SDGs are developed countries, such as the United Kingdom (UK), Australia and Canada, followed by some Western countries, like Spain, France and Portugal, as well as Asian countries, such as Japan and South Korea. In terms of the universal health coverage index, Singapore, Iceland and Sweden scored the highest achievement of health-related SDGs, but the United States of America (USA) showed minimal gains despite its high economic income over the period of 1990–2016 (Fullman et al., 2017). Turkey, Cambodia and China, although not being ranked in top positions, have carried out health reforms and recorded having the most progressive improvement in health coverage since 2000. Strong government commitment to expand government-funded insurance schemes on essential medicines and public health has contributed to a rapid gain in health coverage in China (Fullman et al., 2017). While Turkey and Cambodia are facing challenges on regional instability and weak national insurance system, respectively, developing and least developed countries, such as Afghanistan, Central Africa Republic and Somalia, continue to have the worst healthcare performance due to civil unrest and violence (Fullman et al., 2017). The benefit and impact of this SDG to the elderly population in Hong Kong, with review of how the government, the healthcare profession and the community can and should cooperate to accomplish health improvement and quality of life among elderly, will be presented in the next chapter as a case study.

Goal 4: ensure inclusive and equitable quality education, and promote lifelong learning opportunities for all

SDG 4 is striving for the accomplishment of free, equitable and quality education in primary and secondary schools for all girls and boys, and equal access to affordable tertiary education for all women and men. It also aims to ensure learners acquire knowledge and skills to achieve sustainable development by 2030. To achieve the success of inclusive and equitable quality education, the number of scholarships and qualified teachers through international cooperation for ongoing teacher training and continuing education needs to be expanded globally.

A lack of trained teachers and poor conditions of school sites, as well as the equity issues, are the major challenges in education systems. Latin American countries are still falling behind in educational provision, reflected from their non-significant increase in the priority given to public spending in education (United Nations Educational, Scientific and Cultural Organisation, 2014). The Mexican government has taken many initiatives to implement the SDGs with long-term visions, including improving educational provision and infrastructures. Meeting the demand of educational needs, the 'Schools to 100' programme and the National Educational Infrastructure Certificates improved 10,913 educational facilities across Mexico (Oxford Business Group, 2017). Moreover, the Mexican government has started to research on pedagogies of science, technology, engineering and mathematics (STEM) education and introduced the disciplines of physics, chemistry and mathematics to children and teenagers (Montgomery & Fernández-Cárdenas, 2018). Importantly, 78.2% of the Mexican population aged 3 to 23 had enrolled in the National Education System by 2016 (Mexico Federal Government, 2018).

Goal 5: achieve gender equality and empower all women and girls

SDG 5 targets to eliminate all types of discrimination, including negative stereotypes, both verbal or physical violence, and harmful practice, such as child, early and forced marriage, and female genital mutilation against women and girls (UN, 2021b). SDG 5 aims to eliminate gender inequality by ensuring women and girls equal opportunities for leadership and equal rights to economic resources.

Eliminating traditional patriarchy and sealed social norms can lead to gender equality. Due to the problem of child marriage, many women were married before 18 years old, and this local culture and social customs obviously hinder their future life planning. Moreover, some communities in Kenya and other areas in Africa still have a harmful and traditional practice of female genital mutilation/cutting (FGMC) that causes permanent damage (Achia, 2014). Kenya is one of the successful stories in the efforts to abandon the practice of FGMC as non-governmental organisations (NGOs) in Kenya have been active in promoting social and educational campaigns to achieving health and gender equality (Grose et al., 2019). FGMC has become much less common than in the past three decades, and the government has planned to end it by 2022 (United Nations Children's Fund, 2020).

In particular, women's participation in elections is relatively passive around the world, with the rating of only 23.4% of women joining national parliaments in 2017 (Inter-Parliamentary Union, 2018). Under the influence of SDG 5, positive changes in cultural and social norms have resulted in the promotion of participation of women as voters, candidates and political party leaders. For instance, Argentina, Chile and Ecuador have adopted progressive legislation to promote female political leadership (Inter-Parliamentary Union, 2018).

Goal 6: ensure availability and sustainable management of water and sanitation for all

SDG 6 aims to achieve equitable access to safe and affordable drinking water and available sanitation by 2030. It targets to increase sustainability of water use and improve water quality by reducing pollution and eliminating untreated wastewater in all sectors and facilities. To protect the whole water-related ecosystems, it emphasises the expansion of international cooperation on water and sanitation-related management, including wastewater treatment, and recycle and reuse technologies.

Water demand increases, arising from utilisation in agricultural and industrial development as the populations grow. Meanwhile, some developing countries are having poor water security. For example, Nepal has a high annual rainfall but lacks the congruence between locations of water availability and water need, while Brazil has huge variation on water regulations and underinvestment in upgrades of water infrastructure (Nepal et al., 2021; Victor et al., 2015). The governments of Nepal and Finland have jointly financed the Rural Water Supply and Sanitation Project in Western Nepal, and the Rural Village Water Resources Management Project in remote rural communities in Nepal to provide technical assistance in planning and capacity development of water and sanitation (White et al., 2017). Both projects have significant results in improving the sanitation and domestic water coverage in villages via technology, such as gravity-fed water supply systems, solar water-lift system and hydraulic ram pumps. In Brazil, the federal government has reformed the water policies by revising the National Water Law and adding values to the National Environmental Policy Act (Victor et al., 2015). There are also new concepts of water resource management, including user-pays principles and participatory management. However, water coverage is currently 83.6%, and sanitation does not evolve significantly in some Brazilian cities (da Silva et al., 2021; Dias et al., 2018). More efforts are needed to attain the goals of universal and equitable access to clean water in Brazil.

Goal 7: ensure access to affordable, reliable, sustainable and modern energy for all

SDG 7 aims to guarantee universal access to modern, affordable and reliable energy services by 2030. Energy is an important element to support advancements in health, education and water management. Thus, it has significant influence on the achievement of other related SDGs. To improve energy efficiency and environmental sustainability, it is crucial to increase the share of renewable energy and enhance international cooperation to facilitate research and innovation on clean and renewable energy technologies, such as wind, solar and geothermal.

Some countries have the advantages in innovation and technology, and therefore, they have better developed utilisation of renewable energy. The European Union (EU), the USA and China have their populations relying less on the access to electricity generated by oil usage, and there is a positive trend of using renewable energy for electricity generation (Etxeberria Arano, 2020). For instance, Spain and France have gradually increased the utilisation of renewable energy to 36.8% and 21%, respectively. Notably, Germany and Sweden utilise biomethane (upgraded biogas) generated by waste materials as a form of renewable energy to maintain a friendly environment (Dada & Mbohwa, 2018). The USA also increases the share of renewable energy, but they are slightly lagging behind the EU, while China has a rapid progress in developing renewable energy since the launch of Renewable Energy Law in 2005 (Ji & Zhang, 2019). To reform the energy structure in China, policies and regulations, including pricing system, financial support and quality control, have been steadily promulgated over the past ten years, making China the biggest investor in renewable energy since 2013 (Ji & Zhang, 2019). By the end of 2017, the development on wind, solar and hydroelectric energy contributed to 35.7% of total installed capacity of electric power (Liu, 2019).

Goal 8: promote sustained inclusive and sustainable economic growth, full and productive employment, and decent work for all

Sustaining economic growth and increasing economic productivity through upgrading technology, and promoting innovation and entrepreneurship are targeted in SDG 8. Ending slavery and forced labour are particularly needed in developing countries. Moreover, protecting labour rights and equal pay for work among all women and men are important to sustain employment, decent work and support economic activities.

The economies of the Group of Twenty (G20), which is made up of 19 fastest-growing developed and developing countries and the EU, represent around 80% of the global economic output (Lapinskaitė & Vidžiūnaitė, 2020). Among G20, Japan, Korea, India and China are Asian countries that have occupied three out of the top five countries to have achieved progress in SDG 8. Other developing countries in Asia, such as Thailand, has moved from a low-income to an upper middle–income country in less than a generation. Its economic growth in an average annual rate of 7.5% has helped to decrease poverty rate and improve social security (The World Bank, 2021). Undergoing the structural changes from agriculture to industry, economic reform strategies in Thailand include expanding manufacturing exports, attracting foreign investors, reducing taxes and introducing Thailand 4.0 to develop Thailand into a value-based and innovation-driven economy (Organisation for Economic Co-operation and Development, 2021). Working with the World Bank, the Thailand-World Bank Group Country Partnership Framework is expected to further support Thailand in the improvement of business environment and strengthening of economic institutions in the development of sustainable economic growth (The World Bank, 2021).

Goal 9: build resilient infrastructure, promote inclusive and sustainable industrialisation, and foster innovation

SDG 9 focuses on building resilient infrastructures to support sustainable industrialisation, economic development and innovation. Industrialisation drives economic growth by increasing the employment and GDP, while upgrading infrastructure and retrofit industries allow efficient use of resources. There are also targets of enhancing scientific research and innovation to improve the technological capabilities and domestic technology development in different industrial sectors. To the less developed countries, SDG 9 aims to significantly increase their access to resource, information and communications technology.

The SDG 9 index represents the industrial performance and progress in meeting the targets of SDG 9 in 128 countries, and it measured how a country had achieved the goal of inclusive sustainable industrial development over the period 2000–2016 (Kynčlová et al., 2020). The top five countries were developed countries, including Ireland, Germany, South Korea, Switzerland and Japan. Notably, Ireland ranked from the seventh to the first as a result of their policies of relocating manufacturing activities to local places and lowering corporation tax rates (Kynčlová et al., 2020). For emerging industrial economies, for example Russia, efforts have been made to undergo transformation of the economy from traditional sectors, such as agriculture and fishery, to a modern manufacturing industry based on innovation and technology. Infrastructure development is one of the core elements in Russia's policy agenda in 2024 (Kolmar & Sakharov, 2019). Although substantial works have to be done on the sustainable infrastructure, the Russian Federation has paid specific attention to the treatment of hazardous waste, development of modern healthcare infrastructure, renovation of regional and local roadways, and improvement of digital infrastructure for big data storage (Kolmar & Sakharov, 2019).

Goal 10: reduce inequality within and among countries

SDG 10 is targeting the reduction of inequalities of income as well as those related to age, sex, disability and race within and among countries. Unequal opportunities and inequalities are reduced through the formulation of policies on fiscal, wage and social protection. Migration policies should also be well-managed to promote safe, regular and responsible mobility of people. It again encourages foreign investment to the less developed countries, such as African countries and Small Island Developing States, such as Bahrain, Cuba and Fiji (UN, 2021a). SDG 10 also specifies the reduction of less than 3% of transaction costs of migrant remittances.

Thailand has the highest inequality rate in terms of income disparity and social attributes in Southeast Asia (Pothipala et al., 2020). People who live in rural areas in Thailand experience income and social inequalities as they have lower economic and social opportunities. In addition, patronage relationship is strong in rural agrarians. Apart from the integration of living wage in the Sufficiency Economy Philosophy, the government of Thailand also approved the Social Enterprise Act in 2019 and started to provide grants and loans to encourage the formation of organisations that helped citizens to increase self-sustainability and independence through employment (Pothipala et al., 2020; Yoelao et al., 2021). This type of social enterprises has benefited different social and disadvantaged groups, mainly those who are concerned with agricultures, tourism, and handicraft and garments in Thailand.

Goal 11: make cities and human settlements inclusive, safe, resilient and sustainable

More than half of the world's population are now living in cities, and the importance of setting up safe urban areas is increasing. SDG 11 motivates governments to provide access for all to adequate, safe and affordable living places and basic community services. By enhancing inclusive and sustainable urbanisation, it may significantly reduce the mortality rate. Thus, SDG 11 can avoid direct economic losses that lead to the reduction in GDP. It becomes the guide for inclusive, safe, resilient and sustainable cities, and supports the development of countries with financial and technical assistance (Koch & Ahmad, 2018).

To fulfil this goal, local governments become important stakeholders to identify and quantify the targets, which can indicate the related public policies in the society. For example, in Spain, as a developed country, local governments have identified and calculated the global factors that shall be achieved to meet SDG 11 with the idea "Think globally, act locally". They have prioritised the issues in the improvement of the slum and safe and accessible public spaces, and focused on the importance of daily urban solid waste collection (Martínez-Córdoba et al., 2021). In the Western Pacific area, Australia is a highly urbanised country that has easy access to green spaces and natural environment. The federal government has cooperated with all levels of governments, industry partners, and private and public sectors to build resilient and sustainable cities (Australian Government, 2018). Through the Smart Cities and Suburbs Programme, 3D technologies and energy-efficiency technologies are adopted in urban planning to improve lighting, traffic, waste management and carbon emissions in Australia. The housing and urban infill are also balanced with access to green space for environmental services (Australian Government, 2018). Singapore is another country in the Western Pacific area that has developed good urban planning, with public housing policy being very successful (Lye, 2020; Nubi et al., 2021). The national public housing programme in Singapore accounted for over 70% of residential real estates, and homeownership rate was more than 90% in 2015, with 75% of public housing ownership (Nubi et al., 2021). To promote family ties and racial harmony, unique initiatives in public housing policy are adopted in Singapore. For instance, multigenerational families can get grant and flat allocation priority, and mixture of racial groups are integrated in the new housing flats (Lye, 2020).

Turkey, as a developing country, is also meeting the goal by implementing urbanisation to facilitate people with safe and sustainable life. Under the Strategy Plan of the Istanbul Metropolitan Municipality, local governments of Turkey target to convert slums into regular living. They are performing infrastructure studies to enable urban planning, with the aims to contribute to sustainable environment and waste management, and enable and disseminate services to the disadvantaged groups (Akyildiz, 2017).

Goal 12: ensure sustainable consumption and production patterns

The production of goods and services is important to the improvement of the quality of life, which enhances economic growth and development in the long run. SDG 12 reminds the world that having sustainable and responsible consumption and production patterns can minimise the utilisation of natural resources and potentially toxic materials, and avoid the generation of waste and pollutants that are detrimental to human beings and the environment. This goal encourages participation of companies, manufacturers and suppliers to apply sustainable practices and establish public procurement practices, in accordance with sustainable national policies and priorities. Scientific and technological capacity should be strengthened to support sustainable consumption and production in daily living.

In particular, the 10-Year Framework of Programmes on Sustainable Consumption and Production (10YFP) has been implemented globally. The Swedish government has proposed strategies to help consumers consume sustainably, with measures of supporting education on consumption impacts; promotion of eco-smart behaviour, including sharing economy and eco-labelling; revision to a national waste management plan; penalty for false "green" claims in marketing; and investment on public transport and cycling (Ministry of Finance Sweden, 2016). The Swedish government has also identified the need to build scientific and technological capacity in food production as part of the sustainable consumption measure, and have also adopted sustainable procurement practices in companies and public procurement. Reports had shown that CO_2-differentiated vehicle tax and congestion charges were effective in shaping consumption behaviour in Gothenburg and Stockholm (Chan et at., 2018).

In order to minimise environmental impacts to food systems and nutrition security, sustainable eating has been promoted by the UN, with recommendations including having more plant-based diet, food waste reduction, and focus on seasonal and local food, which is more nutritious and fresher to human bodies and the environment (Food and Agriculture Organisation of the United Nations, 2021). Green diet, one of the ways to sustain food consumption as well as to promote healthy ageing, focuses on a diet rich in plant foods with minimal portions of meat and processed meat, and emphasises the benefits of food origins to be environmentally responsible (Fong et al., 2021). Sweden, Switzerland, Qatar, Norway and Germany have formally incorporated sustainability in their national dietary guidelines (Mouthful, 2020). For example, it is explained that less water waste and greenhouse gas emissions are produced in plant-based food production in the Qatar Dietary Guidelines (The Supreme Council of Health, 2015). The Qatari government emphasises plant-based diet, including whole grain cereals, vegetables and fruits, as one of the key diet recommendations. Similarly, the Norway government suggests that the kind of food we consume impacts not only people's health but also the environment, and they launched a dietary guideline to encourage people to take healthy and eco-smart food choices (Swedish National Food Agency, 2015).

Goal 13: take urgent action to combat climate change and its impacts

SDG 13 aims to reinforce resilience and adaptive capacity in all countries when facing natural disasters and climate-related hazards through the integration of climate change measures into the policies, strategies and national planning. It encourages governments to improve the education system and raises the awareness and institutional capacity in the mitigation, impact reduction and early warning of climate change. Furthermore, it promotes the commitment undertaken by developed countries to help in addressing the needs of developing countries, least developed countries and other small territories to raise their capacity building for effective climate change management.

Nigeria, a developing country, has demonstrated the level of preparedness in achieving SDG 13. The government has proposed two appropriate climate-related policies, the National Climate Change Policy Response Strategy and the National Policy on Environment (Abdullahi, 2020). They have provided training for personnel and experts in capacity building and technology support to combat climate change and in compliance with global commitments. Embracing SDG 13 also requires sufficient financial resources and capacity in the developing and least developed countries. USA and Japan are two of the major contributors to the climate mitigation and adaptation initiatives through the Green Climate Fund, which provides support for reducing greenhouse gases in other developing countries (Green Climate Fund, 2021). In addition, China had the largest performance gaps (30.1%) in achieving SDG 13 (Lafortune & Schmidt-Traub, 2019). Green Development Index System was released for assessing the implementation of ecological civilisation in China (Wang et al., 2020), but the score of SDG 13 was decreased over time (Xu et al., 2020). Therefore, the Chinese government needs to spend more efforts and actions to combat climate change. Apart from the policies in various countries, Airports Council International had introduced an Airport Carbon Accreditation programme to achieve carbon neutrality at various airports (Dube, 2021). More than 300 international airports joined this voluntary programme, and the accredited airports had reduced more than 300,000 tonnes of carbon emission in July 2018–June 2019.

By and large, the provision of finance and technology, together with the interdisciplinary collaboration of stakeholders in all countries, can help to strengthen the resilience to climate-related hazards and enhance the global achievement of SDG 13.

Goal 14: conserve and sustainably use the oceans, seas, and marine resources for sustainable development

This SDG aims to prevent and reduce marine pollution of all kinds, and eliminate marine debris and nutrient pollution. Towards a sustainable ocean economy entails sustainability in ocean management for protection, production and prosperity. It benefits the nature, the economy and the people in the world. Through such sustainable management and protection of marine and coastal ecosystems, it can strengthen oceanic resilience for easier restoration and productivity. Therefore, there are targets to regulate harvesting in the oceans and end overfishing as well as illegal, unreported and unregulated fishing practices, which are detrimental to the biological ecosystem. More research capacity in marine technology is highly encouraged to improve marine biodiversity and promote a healthy and resilient ocean.

Human activities are harming and putting stress on the ecosystem of oceans. To maintain the fish stocks and protect ecological and economic wealth, sustainable small-scale fishing is an important practice to revive the ocean with sustainability (Landin, 2020). Australia performs strongly in designating marine parks in all states and territories with coastal borders. A total of 36% of oceans in Australia is providing long-term conservation of ocean sites (Delany-Crowe et al., 2019). More importantly, the Australian government has proposed policies to balance human economic value of fishermen with conservation, including the management of fish stock numbers in freshwater and ocean waterways, with catch limit, fishing licenses and permits (Delany-Crowe et al., 2019).

Goal 15: protect, restore and promote sustainable use of terrestrial ecosystems; sustainably manage forests; combat desertification; hand halt and reverse land degradation; and halt biodiversity loss

Diverse forms of life on land should be preserved, with targeted efforts to protect, restore and promote the required conservation and sustainable use of terrestrial and freshwater ecosystems. SDG 15 emphasises better management of all types of forests and lands affected by desertification, drought and floods, to reduce biodiversity loss. Countries are urged to integrate ecosystem and biodiversity values in local planning to reduce degradation of natural habitats and halt the loss or extinction of threatened species.

Deforestation and forest degradation occur in many developing countries, such as Indonesia and Brazil. In just about 25 years, forest coverage has substantially decreased by 27,535 hectares (Hiratsuka et al., 2019). The Indonesia government has therefore promoted the concept of social forestry, which refers to a system of forest management involving local communities under Indonesia's Forestry Law. Through the participatory collective action in local communities, sanctions of harvesting and extraction of non-timber forest products are implemented. The establishment of plantations and activities of landscape-level forest conservation had resulted in forest rehabilitation. Improvements to wildlife habitats was reported and wild mammals had been recorded in newly established secondary forest (Hiratsuka et al., 2019). Compared to the developing countries, forest and landscape conservation is well established in developed countries; for example, Canada. Canada contains 30% and 20% of the world's boreal forest and freshwater resources, respectively. In average, 400,000 hectares of provincial forestlands are planted with seedlings to regenerate timber harvesting in Canada, and under provincial and territorial laws, forested areas remain relatively stable due to successful regeneration (Mansuy et al., 2020).

Goal 16: promote peaceful and inclusive societies for sustainable development, provide access to justice for all, and build effective, accountable and inclusive institutions at all levels

Violence of all kinds and related death rates, corruption and bribery must be reduced in the world. By ending all abuse, exploitation, human trafficking or torture of children, SDG 16 motivates the world to provide legal identity for all people, including birth registration. It is important to ensure sustainable and systematic public access to justice, information and protection of basic freedoms, and promote the rule of law at the international level. Globally, prevention of violence and terrorism and crime through close international cooperation should be accomplished.

SDG 16 is one the most challenging goals to achieve, especially in some developing countries where there are issues on governance, human rights and national security. In Africa, corruption remains a severe social and political problem that seriously hinders economic, political and social development. It was indicated that two in five poor Africans paid bribes to get access to public services (Hope, 2021). Most Sub-Saharan African countries, such as Nigeria and Kenya, have ratified the United Nations Convention Against Corruption, which supports anti-corruption and enforcement of punishment, but anti-corruption strategies remain "pending" (Senu, 2020). Peace in these countries cannot be guaranteed. In contrast, based on the 17 SDGs, Egypt has issued Sustainable Development Strategy 2030, emphasising promises of justice, social integration and a better life to Egyptians (El Baradei, 2020). They are making steady progress on decreasing the prison population and increasing birth registration with civil authority. Overall, improvement in the effectiveness of the government and some improvements in both the rule of law and control of corruption are noted (El Baradei, 2020).

Goal 17: strengthen the means of implementation and revitalise the global partnership for sustainable development

SDG 17 is the goal that targets multistakeholder and global partnerships to increase the capacity building of achieving the SDGs at all levels. Developed countries are encouraged to strengthen the domestic resource mobilisation through supporting developing countries to improve their domestic capacity. Developed countries should also coordinate with developing countries in policies making on investment promotion, debt relief and debt restructuring. In terms of technology and innovation, international collaboration on sharing knowledge and exchanging information should be enhanced.

To sustain a society with expertise, knowledge and resources, cross-sector partnerships among different stakeholders, such as businesses, government, civil society, NGOs and universities, play a crucial role (Castillo-Villar., 2020). The formation of G20 has taken the lead in the implementation of SDGs and offered opportunities for coordination of developing countries in international trading, investment, finance, security and global value chains (Fues, 2017). The OECD (2019) identified how G20 had contributed to SDGs by strengthening global partnerships with low-income and developing countries in the aspects of economic, social and environmental collaboration. Some marked collective contributions by G20 include (1) enhancement of international tax cooperation and strengthening of domestic resource mobilisation in developing countries; (2) facilitation of developing countries to gain productivity growth in employment, education and living standard through trading and investment; (3) improvement of the use of natural resources, including water, soils and fossil fuels; (4) assistance in structural transformation in Africa and less developed countries; (5) promotion of gender equality and women's empowerment; and (6) combating of corruptions and promotion of integrity (OECD, 2019). Although facing different challenges, such as financing the management and international commitments, it is believed that G20 can continue to adding substantive value in promoting all SDGs.

Sustainable global impacts

To achieve sustainable developments globally, all governments around the world have the responsibilities to revisit and modify their strategies and policies to align with the 17 SDGs. Adjustment of policy, at times radical reform, should aim at better life for all people in the world. Citizens in various demographic statuses or localities should share equitable rights. Case examples presented above are encouraging and inspiring, as many countries have integrated sustainable development into the relevant government policies and national initiatives, demonstrating breakthroughs and success with impacts all over the world.

The Sustainable Development Report 2021 by the United Nations Sustainable Development Solutions Network had closely observed that the global average SDG Index score for 2020 had gradually decreased from the year before for the first time since the worldwide adoption of the SDGs in 2015.

The new phenomenon is mainly due to increased poverty and unemployment arising from economic setback caused by the COVID-19 pandemic. All the three dimensions of sustainable development, namely economic, social, and environmental, are severely affected by the global health emergency, which is likely to rage for months to come despite the availability of vaccines (United Nations Sustainable Development Solutions Network, 2021). All nations are suffering, while all human beings on earth are fighting very hard to learn to live with the unexpected, somehow harsh, precautious measures and to adapt to the new normal pattern of daily routines.

The chaotic situation in the world had gone worse because of the "economic war" between the United States and China in the past few years. Nonetheless, all governments must not halt the excellent works of sustainable development even in hard times. They should be more committed to making their countries the best place for their people, with pledges to incorporate SDGs in all policies and programmes for the benefit of the people, the society, the country and the world, with the long-term goal of sustainable global impacts. Most importantly, as repeatedly suggested in the SDGs, developed countries should help developing countries, including the least developed countries and Small Island Developing States, with the knowledge and expertise, plus needed resources, to build and strengthen the capacity building of the latter in working towards implementing the global SDG framework. Tested innovations and good practices can be introduced and replicated, with localisation, in other countries to help solve social, economic and environmental problems. Such international collaboration and cooperation in narrowing the gaps among the nations will make the world a happy and healthy place to live in.

References

Abdullahi, A. C. (2020). Level of preparedness of Nigeria on achieving sustainable development goal 13. *ATBU Journal of Environmental Technology*, *13*(2), 119–129.

Achia, T. N. (2014). Spatial modelling and mapping of female genital mutilation in Kenya. *BMC Public Health*, *14*(1), 1–14. https://doi.org/10.1186/1471-2458-14-276

Akyildiz, F. (2017). Local governments in Turkey in the context of SDGs and innovation. In C. M. Hintea, B. A. Moldovan, B. V. Radu, & R. M. Suciu (Eds.), *Transylvanian international conference in public administration*. Cluj-Napoca, Romania.

Atukunda, P., Eide, W. B., Kardel, K. R., Iversen, P. O., & Westerberg, A. C. (2021). Unlocking the potential for achievement of the UN Sustainable Development Goal 2 – 'Zero Hunger' – in Africa: Targets, strategies, synergies and challenges. *Food & Nutrition Research*, *65*. https://doi.org/10.29219/fnr.v65.7686.

Australian Government. (2018). *Report on the implementation of the Sustainable Development Goals*. www.dfat.gov.au/sites/default/files/sdg-voluntary-national-review.pdf

Castillo-Villar, R. G. (2020). Identifying determinants of CSR implementation on SDG 17 partnerships for the goals. *Cogent Business & Management*, 7(1), 1847989. https://doi.org/10.1080/23311975.2020.1847989

Chan, S., Weitz, N., Persson, Å., & Trimmer, C. (2018). *SDG 12: Responsible consumption and production–A review of research needs*. Technical annex to the Formas report Forskning för Agenda 2030: Översikt av forskningsbehov och vägar framåt. Stockholm Environment Institute, Stockholm.

Dada, O., & Mbohwa, C. (2018). Energy from waste: A possible way of meeting goal 7 of the sustainable development goals. *Materials Today: Proceedings*, 5(4), 10577–10584. https://doi.org/10.1016/j.matpr.2017.12.390

da Silva, F. R., Câmara, S. F., Pinto, F. R., Soares, M., Viana, M. B., & De Paula, T. M. (2021). Sustainable development goals against Covid-19: The performance of Brazilian cities in SDGs 3 and 6 and their reflection on the pandemic. *Geography, Environment, Sustainability*, 14(1), 9–16. https://doi.org/10.24057/2071-9388-2020-188

Delany-Crowe, T., Marinova, D., Fisher, M., McGreevy, M., & Baum, F. (2019). Australian policies on water management and climate change: Are they supporting the sustainable development goals and improved health and well-being? *Globalization and Health*, 15(1), 1–15. https://doi.org/10.1186/s12992-019-0509-3

Dhahri, S., & Omri, A. (2020). Foreign capital towards SDGs 1 & 2 – Ending poverty and hunger: The role of agricultural production. *Structural Change and Economic Dynamics*, 53, 208–221. https://doi.org/10.1016/j.strueco.2020.02.004

Dias, C. M., Rosa, L. P., Gomez, J., & D'avignon, A. (2018). Achieving the sustainable development goal 06 in Brazil: The universal access to sanitation as a possible mission. *Anais da Academia Brasileira de Ciências*, 90, 1337–1367. https://doi.org/10.1590/0001-3765201820170590

Dube, K. (2021). Climate action at international airports: An analysis of the Airport Carbon Accreditation Programme. In G. Nhamo, D. Chikodzi, & K. Dube (Eds.), *Sustainable development goals for society vol. 2* (pp. 237–251). Springer, Cham. https://doi.org/10.1007/978-3-030-70952-5_16

El Baradei, L. (2020). Politics of evidence-based policy making: Reporting on SDG 16 in Egypt. *International Journal of Public Administration*, 43(5), 425–440. https://doi.org/10.1080/01900692.2019.1668414

Etxeberria Arano, P. (2020). *Analysis of SDG-7: Energy achievement race in China, EU and USA. ImPACT analysis*. https://academica-e.unavarra.es/handle/2454/37609

Fong, B. Y. F., Chiu, W. K., Chan, W. F. M., & Lam, T. Y. (2021). A review study of a green diet and healthy ageing. *International Journal of Environmental Research and Public Health*, 18(15), 8024. https://doi.org/10.3390/ijerph18158024

Food and Agriculture Organisation of the United Nations. (2021). *Dietary guidelines and sustainability*. www.fao.org/nutrition/education/food-dietary-guidelines/background/sustainable-dietary-guidelines/en/

Fues, T. (2017). *How can the G20 promote the global partnership for sustainable development (SDG 17)?* Rising Powers Quarterly Blog.

Fullman, N., Barber, R. M., Amanuel, A. A., Kalkidan, H. A., Abbafati, C., Abbas, K. M., . . . Murray, C. J. L. (2017). Measuring progress and projecting attainment on the basis of past trends of the health-related sustainable development goals in

188 countries: An analysis from the global burden of disease study 2016. *The Lancet, 390*(10100), 1423–1459. http://doi.org/10.1016/S0140-6736(17)32336-X

Global Times. (2021). *China's poverty eradication worth sharing.* www.globaltimes.cn/page/202102/1216755.shtml

Green Climate Fund. (2021). *Resource mobilisation.* https://www.greenclimate.fund/about/resource-mobilisation/irm

Grose, R. G., Hayford, S. R., Cheong, Y. F., Garver, S., Kandala, N. B., & Yount, K. M. (2019). Community influences on female genital mutilation/cutting in Kenya: Norms, opportunities, and ethnic diversity. *Journal of Health and Social Behavior, 60*(1), 84–100. https://doi.org/10.1177%2F0022146518821870

Hanna, R., & Olken, B. A. (2018). Universal basic incomes versus targeted transfers: Anti-poverty programs in developing countries. *Journal of Economic Perspectives, 32*(4), 201–226. https://doi.org/ 10.1257/jep.32.4.201

Hiratsuka, M., Nakama, E., Satriadi, T., Fauzi, H., Aryadi, M., & Morikawa, Y. (2019). An approach to achieve sustainable development goals through participatory land and forest conservation: A case study in South Kalimantan Province, Indonesia. *Journal of Sustainable Forestry, 38*(6), 558–571. https://doi.org/10.10 80/10549811.2019.1598440

Hope Sr., K. R. (2021). Reducing corruption and bribery in Africa as a target of the sustainable development goals: Applying indicators for assessing performance. *Journal of Money Laundering Control,* 1368–5201. https://10.1108/JMLC-03-2-21-0018

Inter-Parliamentary Union. (2018). *Women in parliament in 2017.* www.ipu.org/resources/publications/reports/2018-03/women-in-parliament-in-2017-year-in-review

Ji, Q., & Zhang, D. (2019). How much does financial development contribute to renewable energy growth and upgrading of energy structure in China? *Energy Policy, 128*, 114–124. https://doi.org/10.1016/j.enpol.2018.12.047

Kabonga, I., Dube, E., Dziva, C., & Chaminuka, N. (2021). Ending extreme poverty (SDG 1) in Chegutu District of Zimbabwe: An analysis of Tsungirirai Welfare Organisation's interventions. In *Sustainable development goals for society vol. 1* (pp. 51–64). Springer, Cham. https://doi.org/10.1007/978-3-030-70948-8_4

Koch, F., & Ahmad, S. (2018). How to measure progress towards an inclusive, safe, resilient and sustainable city? Reflections on applying the indicators of sustainable development goal 11 in Germany and India. In S. Kabisch, F. Koch, E. Gawel, A. Haase, S. Knapp, K. Krellenberg, J. Nivala, & A. Zehnsdorf (Eds.), *Urban transformations: Sustainable urban development through resource efficiency, quality of life and resilience* (pp. 77–90). Springer, Cham. https://doi.org/10.1007/978-3-319-59324-1_5

Kolmar, O., & Sakharov, A. (2019). Prospects of implementation of the UN SDG in Russia. *International Organisations Research Journal, 14*(1), 189–206. http://doi.org/10.17323/1996-7845-2019-01-11

Kynčlová, P., Upadhyaya, S., & Nice, T. (2020). Composite index as a measure on achieving Sustainable Development Goal 9 (SDG-9) industry-related targets: The SDG-9 index. *Applied Energy, 265*, 114755. https://doi.org/10.1016/j.apenergy.2020.114755

Lafortune, G., & Schmidt-Traub, G. (2019). SDG challenges in G20 countries. In J. Walker, A. Pekmezovic, & G. Walker (Eds.), *Sustainable development goals: Harnessing business to achieve the SDGs through finance, technology, and law reform* (pp. 219–234). https://doi.org/10.1002/9781119541851.ch12

Landin, A. S. (2020). Social economy as the means to help achieve the targets of sustainable development goal 14. *Sustainability, 12*(11), 4529. https://doi.org/10.3390/su12114529

Lapinskaitė, I., & Vidžiūnaitė, S. (2020). Assessment of the sustainable economic development goal 8: Decent work and economic growth in G20 countries. *Economics and Culture, 17*(1), 116–125. https://doi.org/10.2478/jec-2020-0011

Liu, J. (2019). China's renewable energy law and policy: A critical review. *Renewable and Sustainable Energy Reviews, 99*, 212–219. https://doi.org/10.1016/j.rser.2018.10.007

Lye, L. H. (2020). *Public housing in Singapore: A success story in sustainable development* (NUS Law Working Paper No. 2020/014). NUS Asia-Pacific Centre for Environmental Law. https://papers.ssrn.com/sol3/papers.cfm?abstract_id=3595956

Mansuy, N., Burton, P. J., Stanturf, J., Beatty, C., Mooney, C., Besseau, P., . . . Lapointe, R. (2020). Scaling up forest landscape restoration in Canada in an era of cumulative effects and climate change. *Forest Policy and Economics, 116*, 102177. https://doi.org/10.1016/j.forpol.2020.102177

Martínez-Córdoba, P. J., Amor-Esteban, V., Benito, B., & García-Sánchez, I. M. (2021). The commitment of Spanish local governments to sustainable development goal 11 from a multivariate perspective. *Sustainability, 13*(3), 1222. https://doi.org/10.3390/su13031222

Mexico Federal Government. (2018). *Voluntary national review for the high-level political forum on sustainable development: Basis for a long-term sustainable development vision in Mexico.* https://sustainabledevelopment.un.org/content/documents/20239Voluntary_National_Review_folder_ENG_WEB.PDF

Ministry of Finance Sweden. (2016). *Strategy for sustainable consumption.* www.government.se/articles/2016/10/strategy-for-sustainable-consumption/

Ministry of Statistics and Programme Implementation. (2021). *Sustainable development goals national indicator framework progress report.* http://mospi.nic.in/sites/default/files/publication_reports/SDG-NIF-Progress2021_March%2031.pdf

Montagnini, F., & Metzel, R. (2017). The contribution of agroforestry to sustainable development goal 2: End hunger, achieve food security and improved nutrition, and promote sustainable agriculture. In F. Montagnini (Ed.), *Integrating landscapes: Agroforestry for biodiversity conservation and food sovereignty* (pp. 11–45). Springer, Cham. https://doi.org/10.1007/978-3-319-69371-2_2

Montgomery, C., & Fernández-Cárdenas, J. M. (2018). Teaching STEM education through dialogue and transformative learning: Global significance and local interactions in Mexico and the UK. *Journal of Education for Teaching, 44*(1), 2–13. https://doi.org/10.1080/02607476.2018.1422606

Mouthful. (2020). *Which countries have included sustainability within their national dietary guidelines?* https://themouthful.org/article-sustainable-dietary-guidelines

Nepal, S., Neupane, N., Belbase, D., Pandey, V. P., & Mukherji, A. (2021). Achieving water security in Nepal through unravelling the water-energy-agriculture nexus.

International Journal of Water Resources Development, 37(1), 67–93. https://doi. org/10.1080/07900627.2019.1694867

Nubi, T. G., Anderson, I., Lawanson, T., & Oyalowo, B. (2021). *Housing and SDGs in urban Africa.* Springer, Singapore. https://doi.org/10.1007/978-981-33-4424-2

Organisation for Economic Co-operation and Development. (2019). *G20 contribution to the 2030 Agenda.* www.oecd.org/g20/topics/agenda-2030-development/G20-SDG-Report.pdf

Organisation for Economic Co-operation and Development. (2021). *OECD investment policy reviews: Thailand.* OECD Investment Policy Reviews, OECD Publishing, Paris, https://doi.org/10.1787/c4eeee1c-en

Oxford Business Group. (2017). *Major reforms in Mexico to improve standards in educational system.* https://oxfordbusinessgroup.com/overview/back-school-major-reforms-are-set-improve-standards-across-system

Pernechele, V., Balié, J., & Ghins, L. (2018). *Agricultural policy incentives in sub-Saharan Africa in the last decade (2005–2016): Monitoring and Analysing Food and Agricultural Policies (MAFAP) synthesis study* (No. 2143–2019–4790). https://doi.org/10.22004/ag.econ.296658

Pothipala, V., Keerasuntonpong, P., & Cordery, C. (2020). Alleviating social and economic inequality? The role of social enterprises in Thailand. *Journal of Accounting & Organisational Change, 17*(1), 50–70. http://doi.org/10.1108/JAOC-09-2020-0127

The Supreme Council of Health. (2015). *Qatar dietary guidelines.* www.fao.org/3/az908e/az908e.pdf

Senu, O. (2020). A critical assessment of anti-corruption strategies for economic development in sub-Saharan Africa. *Development Policy Review, 38*(5), 664–681. https://doi.org/10.1111/dpr.12442

Swedish National Food Agency. (2015). *Healthy and eco-smart dietary recommendations.* www.oneplanetnetwork.org/initiative/healthy-and-eco-smart-zdietary-recommendations-swedish-national-food-agency

United Nations. (2021a). *Small island developing states.* https://sustainabledevelopment.un.org/topics/sids/list

United Nations. (2021b). *Ensure healthy lives and promotion well-being for all at all ages.* https://sdgs.un.org/goals/goal3

United Nations Children's Fund. (2020). *A profile of female genital mutilation in Kenya.* https://reliefweb.int/sites/reliefweb.int/files/resources/Profile-of-FGM-in-Kenya-English_2020.pdf

United Nations Educational, Scientific and Cultural Organisation. (2014). *Regional report about education for all in Latin America and the Caribbean: Global education for all meeting Muscat, Oman, May 12th and 14th of 2014.* www.unesco.org/new/fileadmin/MULTIMEDIA/HQ/ED/ED_new/pdf/LAC-GEM-2014-ENG.pdf

United Nations Sustainable Development Solutions Network. (2021). *Sustainable development report 2021.* https://s3.amazonaws.com/sustainabledevelopment.report/2021/2021-sustainable-development-report.pdf

Victor, G., Almeida, P., & Wong, L. (2015). Water management policy in Brazil. *SSRN, 21*. https://doi.org/10.2139/ssrn.2670847

Wang, Y., Lu, Y., He, G., Wang, C., Yuan, J., & Cao, X. (2020). Spatial variability of sustainable development goals in China: A provincial level evaluation. *Environmental Development, 35*, 100483. https://doi.org/10.1016/j.envdev.2019.100483

White, P., Rautanen, S.-L., & Nepal, P. R. (2017). Operationalising the right to water and sanitation and gender equality via appropriate technology in rural Nepal. In M. Garrido Villareal (Ed.), *Human rights and technology: The 2030 agenda for sustainable technology* (pp. 217–239). University of Peace, Costa Rica.

The World Bank. (2021). *The world bank in Thailand.* www.worldbank.org/en/country/thailand/overview#1

Xu, Z., Chau, S. N., Chen, X., Zhang, J., Li, Y., Dietz, T., . . . Liu, J. (2020). Assessing progress towards sustainable development over space and time. *Nature, 577*(7788), 74–78. https://doi.org/10.1038/s41586-019-1846-3

Yoelao, D., Sombatwattana, P., & Mohan, K. P. (2021). Development and validation of the sufficiency living wage scale for workers in Thailand. *Thailand and The World Economy, 39*(1), 23–38.

2 Ageing and Sustainable Development Goal 3 in Hong Kong

Sustainable Development Goal 3: ensure healthy lives and promote well-being for all at all ages

Introduction

Nowadays, more people are living healthier lives than in the past decade. Nevertheless, people are still suffering needlessly from preventable diseases, and too many people are dying prematurely. Overcoming diseases and ill health will require concerted and sustained efforts, focusing on population groups and regions that have been neglected. In many regions of the world, populations have grown older. In 2020, 9% of the global population was above 65 years old, and it had been projected to reach 16% in 2050 (Jarzebski et al., 2021). Hong Kong is no exception in facing the fast pace of ageing population due to extended lifespan, decreased fertility rate and advanced healthcare technology. The life expectancy in Hong Kong in 2019 was 84.9 years and was the highest life expectancy around the world (United Nations Development Programme, 2020). The 2020 COVID-19 pandemic is devastating health systems globally and threatens health outcomes already achieved. Countries need comprehensive health strategies and increased spending on health to meet urgent needs and protect local citizens, while a global coordinated effort is needed to support countries in need.

Compared to other age groups, older people, as the vulnerable group, have a high prevalence of comorbidity and disabilities, associated with experiences and specific challenges related to access to health, personal and home safety, mobility, and capacity to recover from natural disasters. They need sufficient health services to maintain health and to manage serious and continuing chronic illnesses. Therefore, strengthening the prevention of diseases and health service delivery for older people should receive more attention in all countries and regions to achieve healthy ageing. The relationship between health and ageing is inevitable. The COVID-19 pandemic has shown how

DOI: 10.4324/9781003220169-2

older people are facing the threats of developing severe illnesses (World Health Organization, 2021). To improve and relieve the burden of the ageing population, the Hong Kong Special Administrative Region (HKSAR) government has established and launched various strategies and regulations to combat this critical problem. Sustainable Development Goal 3 aims to ensure healthy lives and promote well-being at all ages, with 13 targets. This chapter will discuss how SDG 3 could benefit the ageing population and review how the governments, the healthcare profession and the community can and should cooperate to accomplish health improvement and quality of life among the elderly in Hong Kong, as a case study, with discussion on preventions of communicable diseases and non-communicable diseases (NCDs), universal health coverage, and investment in research and development.

Prevention of communicable diseases

Target 3.3 recommends to end the epidemics of AIDS, tuberculosis, malaria and neglected tropical diseases; and combat hepatitis, waterborne diseases and other communicable diseases by 2030. Incidences of malaria, tropical diseases and waterborne diseases are rather insignificant in Hong Kong, though the older generation had unpleasant experience with these communicable diseases in their early childhood. The prevalence of the five types of hepatitis cases remains relatively low, with a total number of 161 cases in 2020 (Centre for Health Protection, 2020b). Further improvements are expected with the Hong Kong Viral Hepatitis Action Plan 2020–2024 in combating hepatitis. The incidences of AIDS and tuberculosis are both under control and show a declining rate in Hong Kong. However, as the population is ageing, acquired immunodeficiency syndrome (AIDS) and tuberculosis in the vulnerable age group can be worrying without appropriate prevention or interventions.

Human immunodeficiency virus (HIV) spreads through unprotected sex, transfusions of unscreened blood and contaminated needles. It will infect people daily, live and weaken an individual's immune system that they become more prone to serious opportunistic infections (Centre for Health Protection, 2017). If not treated properly, it can become AIDS, the most severe phase of HIV infection. It is estimated that there are 36.7 million people living with HIV (PLHIV) and 5.8 million people aged 50 years above are living with HIV, representing 17% of all adults aged 15 years and over who are living with HIV (Bhatta et al., 2020). In Hong Kong, the number of HIV infection cases gradually decreased in the past few years, with a cumulative total of 10,886 cases as of the first quarter of 2021. In 2019, around 23% of people living with HIV were aged 50 and above (Department of

Health, 2021a; Virtual AIDS Office of Hong Kong, 2021b). The cumulative cases of AIDS increased from 2,118 in 2019 to 2,230 in 2020, and around 40% of people living with AIDS were aged 50 or above in 2019 (Department of Health, 2021a). Men who have sex with men (MSM) had an increasing trend in HIV infection between 2011 and 2015, but it remained stable in the past years in Hong Kong (Department of Health, 2021a). Since the first recognised HIV case reported in 1985 in Hong Kong, the Virtual AIDS Office of Hong Kong was established as a central office for four programmes, namely the Red Ribbon Centre, HIV Clinical Team, AIDS Hotline and HIV Testing Service, and Surveillance Office (Virtual AIDS Office of Hong Kong, 2021a). Educational programmes and research on HIV/AIDS are conducted by the Red Ribbon Centre to increase the community's response to HIV and AIDS. Moreover, the Hong Kong AIDS Foundation provides support services, such as treatment, employment and counselling, for all PLHIV (Hong Kong AIDS Foundation, 2018).

Although most of the patients are diagnosed between the age of 30 and 39, there are people aged 50 who are infected with HIV/AIDS, indicating a demand in elderly service for HIV (Department of Health, 2021a). Proactive involvement of community organisations in Hong Kong has strengthened the scope of HIV and AIDS programmes in meeting the needs of more diverse populations. Different organisations have worked closely with the healthcare profession and academia, community partners, and relevant government departments to reinforce the response to zero new infections of HIV and AIDS. For instance, the Hong Kong Advisory Council on AIDS (ACA), formed in 1990, adopts a broad-based, participatory and integrated approach to formulate strategies for prevention, care and control of AIDS (Hong Kong Advisory Council on AIDS, 2016). Although not prioritised, the latest HIV/AIDS Strategies for Hong Kong 2017–2021 recognised some needs for PLHIV, including (1) strengthening support for long-term side effects from medications, (2) staff training for residential elderly care home, (3) monitoring rejection of PLHIV in elderly home, (4) providing physiological and psychological health support, (5) helping elderly MSM come to terms with their homosexuality, and (6) increasing services for elderly MSM needs (Hong Kong Advisory Council on AIDS, 2016). The outcomes of these strategies are yet to be measured and evaluated, but Hong Kong is on track on tackling AIDS.

Surpassing HIV/AIDs, tuberculosis still accounts for the highest mortality arising from any infectious diseases worldwide, causing 1.5 million deaths in 2018 (Harding, 2020). Tuberculosis is spread through the air, and the bacteria usually attack the lungs but can also affect other parts of the body, such as the kidney and spine (Drug Office, 2014). Similar to some other diseases, tuberculosis is widely known as a disease of poverty that affects the population more heavily in developing countries, such as Haiti, Pakistan and the Philippines (Tam et al., 2018). The incidence rate of tuberculosis in Hong Kong is well-controlled. It is projected that the infectious cases will decrease by only around 60%, not 80%, as targeted by the End TB Strategy (Tam et al., 2018). However, higher prevalence of tuberculosis in older adults was reported, with people aged 60 or above accounting for more than 55% of notifications in 2020 in Hong Kong (Centre for Health Protection, 2020b). It was also found that the mortality of hospitalised patients was due to delayed diagnosis and treatment, and there was a higher risk of reactivation, resulting in high prevalence of latent infection among older adults, particularly in residential care homes (Chong et al., 2019; Tam et al., 2018).

The Tuberculosis and Chest Service (TB&CS) of the Department of Health has monitored likely infectious cases and provided guidelines on handling infectious cases in the community. It also conducts contact screening to facilitate early identifications and diagnosis. Working with the government, the Hong Kong Tuberculosis, Chest and Heart Diseases Association (HKTCHA) had started to promote and encourage research and experimental work on the prevention, diagnosis, treatment and any related aspects of chest, heart and lung diseases since 1940 (Hong Kong Tuberculosis, Chest and Heart Diseases Association, 2021).

Despite the efforts put on combating tuberculosis, it is criticised that there is a lack of clear strategy and timeline for specific goals in tuberculosis control and elimination in Hong Kong. The current treatment measures, passive screening and directly observed treatment, short-course (DOTS) are insufficient in preventing latent tuberculosis infection (LTBI) (Chong et al., 2019). Chong et al. (2019) indicated that there were no practical programmes for LTBI screening or treatment; reactivation cases among high-risk elderly group, accounting for most of the tuberculosis cases in Hong Kong, could not be adequately controlled. As a community programme, it has been suggested to prioritise LTBI treatment for elderly in elderly care homes and to closely monitor for potential adverse side effects (Chong et al., 2019). In order to achieve the SDGs by 2030, improved screening programmes are required, paying more attention to older adults.

In response to target 3.3 regarding ageing, the prevention of communicable diseases in residential care homes for the elderly (RCHEs) in Hong Kong is vital in minimising the risks of chronic diseases and the chance of hospitalisation, with the objective to alleviate the social burden and shorten the waiting time for RCHEs. "Guidelines on Prevention of Communicable Diseases in Residential Care Homes for the Elderly" was published by the Department of Health (Department of Health, 2019). This guideline provides comprehensive information about the detection, prevention and infection control of communicable diseases for the staff. The implementation of the guidelines can significantly promote the infection control in residential care homes. Availability of alcohol-based hand rub and diluted bleach solution was significantly increased from 2006 to 2014 (Wong et al., 2019). However, insufficient training on infection control for staff in residential care homes at the initiation and during employment was found to be due to inadequate manpower (Lee et al., 2017). To improve staff training in residential care homes, the government should provide more resources for staff training to maintain the standard of infection control in residential care homes.

Prevention and treatment for non-communicable diseases

Non-communicable diseases are the major causes of death in Hong Kong, accounting for over 55% of the registered deaths (Department of Health, 2018a). Cancers, pneumonia and heart diseases were the leading causes of death among Hong Kong citizens aged 65 or above in 2019 (Centre for Health Protection, 2020a). The death rate for cancers, pneumonia and heart diseases per 100,000 of the Hong Kong population aged 65 or above were 784.7, 661.1 and 380.6, respectively. In comparison, in Japan, another longevity country, the death rate for cancers, pneumonia and heart diseases per 100,000 of the population aged 65 or above were 920.2, 539.6 and 261.4 in 2019 (Statistics of Japan, 2021). The figures for pneumonia and heart diseases were better in Japan.

In target 3.4 of SDG 3, the main objective is to reduce one-third of premature mortality caused by non-communicable disease by prevention and treatment. The Hong Kong SAR government had launched two strategic frameworks to prevent and control the non-communicable diseases in 2008 and 2018, respectively (Department of Health, 2008, 2018c). The first strategic framework provided the scope and direction for different stakeholders to prevent and control non-communicable diseases, while the second framework listed some detailed targets and indicators to be achieved by 2025 based on the recommendations from the World Health Organization. It contained six goals, namely, engaging the population in promoting their own, their families' and their communities' health; preventing the onset of non-communicable diseases; reducing the progression and complications of non-communicable diseases; and reducing avoidable hospital admissions. To achieve the goals, six strategic directions were promulgated: (1) to support new and strengthen current health promotion activities, (2) to generate effective information that guide action across the disease pathway, (3) to foster engagement between all stakeholders, (4) to build capacity and capability to combat non-communicable diseases, (5) to ensure the healthcare sector is responsive to the challenges of non-communicable diseases, and (6) to strengthen the health-promoting legislation. Partnership, environment, outcome-focused, population-based intervention, life-course approach and empowerment were the key elements in the implementation of the 2008 framework. In fact, the unconditional probability of dying between the ages of 30 and 70 from cardiovascular diseases, cancers, diabetes or chronic respiratory diseases has been declining steadily. It shows that premature mortality from non-communicable diseases is reducing. To take these results further, some concrete targets with actions were proposed in the second framework, such as cancer screening, cancer research and development, primary care development, fostering of public-private partnership, and strengthening of non-communicable diseases surveillance (Department of Health, 2018c). In the following sections, measures implemented to prevent non-communicable diseases will be discussed.

Cancers

Cancers are the leading causes of death among the elderly. The two most common cancers in Hong Kong were colorectal cancer and lung cancer in 2018 (Hong Kong Cancer Registry, 2020). Colorectal cancer is found to be a disease ideal for mass screening, partly because early detection of colorectal cancer is highly treatable (Ng & Wong, 2013). The screening with faecal occult blood test and colonoscopy can reduce the mortality of colorectal cancer by up to 53%. Faecal occult blood test is an inexpensive and widely used screening test for colorectal cancer. Colonoscopy, with a high sensitivity, is the procedure used in the final assessment and diagnosis of colorectal cancer. In Hong Kong, the Colorectal Cancer Screening Programme was piloted in September 2016 to give subsidy to older adults aged 61 to 75 who were receiving screening services in the private sector. The programme was expanded to cover eligible persons aged 50 to 75 in August 2018. Eligible older adults are initially assessed by primary care doctors. Once the result of the faecal occult blood test is positive, consultation and referral for colonoscopy will be arranged. The 2016 pilot programme was evaluated in terms of changes in awareness, attitude, perception, practice and satisfaction of colorectal cancer screening among users, non-users and service providers (Chan et al., 2020). Different stakeholders were satisfied and had positive attitude about the pilot programme. Nevertheless, the insufficient technical support and unclear procedures were the main concern for service improvement. Chan et al. (2020) had suggested that more detailed information and educational interventions were vital for the increase in participation of screening and reduction of colorectal cancer incidence. Huang et al. (2020) had indicated that interventions with perceived behavioural control and behavioural intention could enhance the uptake of colorectal cancer screening in Hong Kong. Providing more concrete and practical information, and increasing the accessibility of services for older adults may improve the participation and coverage of this population programme.

The reduction of cancer mortality rate and the prevalence of tobacco use are proposed in targets 3.4 and 3.a of SDG 3. Lung cancer is the most common cancer for elderly male aged 65 or above (Hong Kong Cancer Registry, 2020). Lung cancer and pattern of smoking among the elderly are worth close attention. The incidence rates of lung cancer per 100,000 Hong Kong citizens were 71.2 for aged 45 to 64 and 271.2 for aged 65 or above in 2018, showing a very obvious and strong correlation to old age. Moreover, mortality rate of lung cancer per 100,000 persons were 222.6 for aged 65 or above in 2018 (Hong Kong Cancer Registry, 2021). Smoking and environmental tobacco smoke, second-hand smoking, or even third-hand smoking are the most important risk factors for lung cancer (Chan-Yeung et al., 2003; Li et al., 2016; Sheng et al., 2018; Tse et al., 2011). Smoking cessation is associated with a decline in the risk and mortality of lung cancer (Tse et al., 2011; Tse et al., 2018; Joseph et al., 2018). In Hong Kong, there are different programmes, interventions and regulations on smoking cessation. The Smoking (Public Health) Ordinance (Cap. 371) restricts the sales of tobacco products and tobacco advertisements in printed publications. The ordinance was amended to extend the non-smoking areas to cover designated indoor areas, such as schools, hospitals, restaurants and public outdoor places, including public transport (Tobacco and Alcohol Control Office, 2021). Moreover, tobacco taxation was significantly increased by 137% from 2009 to 2014, which accounted for about 60% of the average cigarette retail price (Hong Kong Council on Smoking and Health, 2021b). These government actions were found to play an important role in tobacco control, particularly in adolescents and young adults (Apollonio et al., 2021; Cobiac et al., 2015; Verguet et al., 2017). The Elderly Smoking Cessation Promotion Project was launched in 2012 by the Hong Kong Council on Smoking and Health (COSH) to promote smoke-free messages to the elderly through health talks, visits to elderly centres and community activities (Hong Kong Council on Smoking and Health, 2021a). Nevertheless, the daily smoking prevalence among Hong Kong citizens aged 60 or above had remained around 9% from 2011 to 2020, indicating the tobacco control for elderly might be ineffective or at least had little positive impact (Census and Statistics Department, 2011, 2020b). However, previous studies had found that smoking cessation was associated with age, which indicates that older smokers would be more prepared to quit smoking, possibly because of health concern (Abdullah et al., 2006; Qiu et al., 2020). To encourage more elderly people to quit smoking, information on the negative consequence and sharing of successful examples of smoking cessation should help to motivate the elderly to quit smoking. Hopefully, the mortality rate of lung cancer may be reduced.

Diabetes

Diabetes is often associated with increased risk of common non-communicable diseases, such as heart and cerebrovascular diseases. The prevalence of diabetes is associated with increasing age. In 2014/2015, 0.9%, 7.7% and 22.7% of Hong Kong citizens aged 35 to 44, 55 to 64 and 75 to 84, respectively, had been diagnosed of diabetes (Department of Health, 2017). To improve the incidence and health management of diabetes among Hong Kong residents, several programmes and frameworks have been established. Patient Empowerment Programme for patients with diabetes was launched in 2010. This programme was a structured diabetes education programme in the primary care setting through the collaboration of NGOs and the Hospital Authority, with the aims of increasing self-management skills, knowledge of diseases and lifestyle modification for patients (Lian et al., 2017; Wong et al., 2016a). Delaying the initial hospitalisation, reducing the rate of the general outpatient clinic and hospital services, and improving clinical outcomes were identified in the diabetic patients who had participated in Patient Empowerment Programme (Wong et al., 2016a, 2016b). In addition, the cost effectiveness of this programme was evaluated, and it was found that the cost of the programme could be covered by the reduction of utilisation of health services among the patients (Lian et al., 2017). Therefore, educational programme for patients is cost-effective in diabetes management. Furthermore, the Food and Health Bureau had developed the "Hong Kong Reference Framework for Diabetes Care for Adults in Primary Care Settings" (Food and Health Bureau, 2018), which provides an evidence-based reference for healthcare professionals on the screening, diagnosis, prevention and management of diabetes. It requires doctors to perform extra assessments, such as glycaemic and blood pressure control, annual assessment, and foot education. Nonetheless, the adoption of this framework among primary care doctors was high, but the extra assessments were suboptimal (Wong et al., 2016c). Essentially, people who are aged 45 or above, or with risk factors for diabetes, are recommended to screen for fasting glucose or glycosylated haemoglobin, commonly known as HbA1c. This can lead to early detection and appropriate interventions of diabetes. With the high adoption rate of the framework, prevention of diabetes in the community can be achieved, particularly in the elderly population.

Promotion of mental health and well-being

Mental conditions are alarming to all people in the world because it is difficult to discover them and to recover from them. Promotion of mental health and well-being is expressed in target 3.4 and is important in the early detection, prevention and management of mental illnesses. To achieve this target, reduction of suicide mortality rate is the major indicator since mental disorders, such as depression and anxiety, are often related to suicide ideation. The suicide rate among elderly is more than those of any other age groups, implying that mental health among the elderly is of much more concern (Chiu et al., 2004; Sun et al., 2012). In Hong Kong, the suicide rate of citizens aged 65 or above were 23.6, 24.5 and 21 per 100,000 population in 2015, 2017 and 2019, respectively (Centre for Suicide Research and Prevention, 2020).

Deterioration in physical health, lack of financial support, sense of loneliness and social exclusion were often associated with depressive symptoms among Hong Kong elderly people (Hung et al., 2016; Kwong et al., 2020; Lee & Chou, 2019; Sau Po Centre on Ageing, 2019). To enhance the awareness of the elderly and their caregivers about the importance of mental health, the Elderly Health Service of Department of Health have conducted health talks, conducted seminars and disseminated related information in the mass media (Food and Health Bureau, 2017). On-site education and training are delivered to the community and residential care settings. Besides, the Social Welfare Department provides community support services, which are not only physical assistance but also emotional support to the elderly. The Hong Kong Family Welfare Society, a NGO, also provides community care and support services to the elderly, including psychiatric consultation service and mental health group for older adults (Hong Kong Family Welfare Society, 2021). These services can facilitate and encourage the elderly and caregivers to identify the source of stress and understand how to handle it.

The mental health status of the elderly is a main concern during the COVID-19 pandemic. Social isolation, fear of being infected by COVID-19 and sudden change in financial situation had a negative impact on the mental health of the population (Fong et al., 2020). The level of stress, anxiety and depressive symptoms were found to have increased during COVID-19 (Zhao et al., 2020). After the onset of the COVID-19 pandemic, loneliness, anxiety and insomnia had significantly increased in older adults, aged 60 or above, who suufered from at least two chronic conditions (Wong et al., 2020). A recent COVID-19 study in Hong Kong put forward that reducing loneliness could effectively reduce the mental illness, and this requires the joint effort of clinicians, caregivers and other stakeholders (Tso & Park, 2020). Hence, close cooperation among the government, local community and healthcare professionals should be strengthened to deal with the mental health problem of the elderly during the pandemic. The use of telecommunication is an alternative to maintain social life and receive health information, but the limited access of internet and digital devices among the elderly, and limited digital literacy skills are the major barriers (Lau et al., 2021). The HKSAR government has called for information technology support for the elderly in the Phase 1 Mental Health Initiatives Funding Scheme for the implementation of mental health projects by service providers and NGOs (The Government of the Hong Kong Special Administrative Region, 2021).

Universal health coverage

A number of previous health studies have found that poverty affects the accessibility of regular sources of primary care. People of low income cannot receive equal health care in some societies (Chung et al., 2019; Flores-Flores et al., 2018; Fujita et al., 2016). Affordability is one of the main determinants of healthcare access (Peters et al., 2008). Therefore, low-income individuals are less likely to access suitable health care. To ensure equally and equitably accessible health care for all individuals, target 3.8 suggests universal health coverage, including financial risk protection, access to quality essential healthcare services, and access to safe, effective, quality and affordable essential medicines and vaccines for all. In Hong Kong, the government provides various welfare schemes, such as Comprehensive Social Security Assistance Scheme, Old Age Allowance and Old Age Living Allowance, to meet the basic needs of the elderly. Poverty among the elderly in Hong Kong is still a serious social issue because the poverty rate of people aged 65 or above had remained at more than 30% from 2009 to 2019 (Census and Statistics Department, 2020a). Lee and Chou (2016) have revealed that going to work is the major way of preventing poverty among the elderly in Hong Kong. Luckily, the elderly and the poor in Hong Kong have equitable access to health care irrespective of their socio-economic status.

The healthcare system in Hong Kong operates in a dual track system encompassing the public and private sectors. The public share in total health expenditure accounted for 53.5% in 2019/20, while 67.6%, 9.1% and 6.9% were distributed to curative care, long-term care and preventive care, respectively (Food and Health Bureau, 2021). All Hong Kong citizens pay a relatively low cost for public medical service: HK$180 for each attendance at the accident and emergency department, and HK$75 for the admission fee of inpatient service. The fee for elderly patients who have low income or few assets, low-income patients and chronically ill patients can be waived.

Therefore, elderly patients would naturally tend to rely on public health services due to affordability. This was shown by the increased attendance at the accident and emergency department, specialist outpatient clinics and patient days among aged 65 or above from 2015–2016 to 2019–2020 (Hospital Authority, 2021). To ease the over reliance on public health services among the elderly, the Elderly Health Care Voucher Scheme was initially implemented in 2009. Elderly people over 65 years of age can receive an annual healthcare voucher in the amount of HK$2,000, with accumulation of the amount up to the limit of HK$8,000, to pay for some private health services, such as services in medical consultations, Chinese medicine, dental service and physiotherapy (Health Care Voucher, 2021). The elderly patients are encouraged to utilise private primary health services, such as health assessments. However, the voucher scheme may not meet the initial objective of providing financial incentives for the elderly to use private health services, particularly in disease prevention and management. The elderly would prefer to spend the voucher in a one-off episodic acute care or save it up for later use rather than spend it for the prevention and management of diseases (Fung et al., 2020; Lai et al., 2017). To improve the elderly voucher scheme, public education and social marketing on the use of the voucher, especially for the elderly, are needed to raise the awareness of the scheme and services in the prevention and management of diseases, thus helping to remove knowledge barriers.

Community health services are established for the local people, where they live. Such services are essential in providing universal health coverage to all residents. In Hong Kong, elderly health centres are operating in all eighteen districts. These health centres mainly provide primary care services to enrolled elderly, including physical examinations and health assessment and prevention. However, less than 4% of the elderly population were members of the elderly health centres from 2017 to 2019 (Legislative Council Secretariat, 2020). It reflects that the elderly health centres can only cover very few of the elderly population in Hong Kong, and the community care services fall behind the demand. According to the Legislative Council Secretariat (2021), community care services refer to long-term care services provided for the elderly in the community or at home. There are four types of community care services, namely home-based, centre-based, respite services for carers and preventive services for the least impaired elderly. The waiting time of subsidised community care services for elderly was six to ten months in June 2021. To shorten the waiting time for subsidised services, the government had launched a Pilot Scheme on Community Care Service Voucher for the Elderly in 2013. This scheme would offer vouchers for the elderly to purchase service packages on centre-based, home-based or mixed mode; and they were required to pay the co-payment amount of the services. Financial conditions, family caregiving support and financial supports, and attitudes towards the voucher scheme were found to contribute to the willingness to pay for the scheme among older people (Fu et al., 2018). Therefore, it may not attract older adults with a low socio-economic status to join this voucher scheme. There are also other challenges in the development and provision of elderly services in Hong Kong (Yu et al., 2019). At the same time, the supply of subsidised residential care services for the elderly cannot meet the social needs. The average waiting time for Care-and-Attention Home and Nursing Homes, which are the two main subsidised residential care services, were 23 months and 33 months between 2007 and 2018 (Lam, 2020). Around 5% to 10% of applicants withdrew their requests, while 15% to 30% of applicants on the waiting list died during the waiting period (Lam, 2020; Legislative Council Secretariat, 2017). The government needs to resolve the scanty and grossly insufficient supply of subsidised residential care services. They can purchase more places from private homes, to ensure healthy lives and promote well-being for the elderly.

Affordable essential medicines and vaccines for all

In addition to the "access to safe, effective, quality and affordable essential medicines and vaccines for all" deliberated in target 3.8 that emphasises universal health coverage, target 3.b recommends the support of research and development of vaccines and medicines for communicable and non-communicable diseases.

Research funding in health and medicine

Funding support is essential in all kinds of research and can motivate researchers to conduct quality, innovative and insightful studies, which are beneficial to the local community and the society at large, resulting in better and healthy lives and well-being. The HKSAR government provides funding sources, including the Health and Medical Research Fund (HMRF), to researchers from tertiary institutions, hospitals and non-government organisations. The HMRF was established in 2011 by the Food and Health Bureau to support health and medical research to improve public health, strengthen the health system and promote clinical excellence. The latest injection of $1.3 billion by the government in 2021 aimed to sustain the operation of the HMRF and to enhance its funding scope (Research Fund Secretariat, 2021). Over 830 projects were funded by the HMRF since 2016–2017, and the topics covered health promotion, effectiveness of health interventions and advancement of screening and prevention. Some of the funded projects were beneficial to the elderly, such as developing community exercise programmes for the elderly to prevent diabetic shoulder problems. Apart from the HMRF, the Hong Kong government had allocated HK$500 million to operate the Chinese Medicine Development Fund since 2019 (Chinese Medicine Development Fund, 2021). In Hong Kong, both Chinese medicine and Western medicine are available, but the general acceptance of Chinese medicine is largely different from Western medicine. The public perception of traditional Chinese medicine is strongly affected by the perceived insufficient scientific evidence (Sun et al., 2017). However, older persons are more likely to use Chinese medicine for their illnesses (Chan & Tsang, 2018). The establishment of the Chinese Medicine Development Fund aims to promote the development of the Chinese medicine by enhancing public knowledge and scientific support of Chinese medicine.

Access to essential medicines

Providing affordable and quality medicines to local residents is a prerequisite in ensuring universal health coverage for the population. Resources allocation on drugs is the means to achieve this target. In Hong Kong, the total drug expenditure of the Hospital Authority, which manages all public hospitals, had risen from HK$4.94 billion in 2013–2014 to HK$8.62 billion in 2020–2021 (Legislative Council Secretariat, 2019; Panel on Health Services, 2021). The Drug Formulary is implemented by the Hospital Authority to ensure equitable access of drugs by patients. The Drug Formulary categorised drugs into four main groups: general drugs, special drugs, self-financed items (SFIs) with safety net and SFIs without safety net. General drugs are drugs selected on the basis of cost-effectiveness and are available for general use. Special drugs are used under specific clinical conditions with specific specialist authorisation. Both general drugs and special drugs are essential medicines provided at standard fees, which are very low and affordable for most of the local citizens. In the Drug Formulary, there were over 880 and 410 general drugs and special drugs, respectively, as of January 2021 (Panel on Health Services, 2021). SFIs with and without Safety Net are expensive drugs that require patients to pay individually. There is a safety net provided by the Community Care Fund Medical Assistance Programmes to give subsidy to patients with financial difficulties. This arrangement has made expensive drugs affordable and accessible to the majority of the patients, particularly the elderly. Nonetheless, the common practice of prescribing multiple medications, also known as polypharmacy, is a concern and is the main cause of potentially inappropriate medication associated with untoward side effects among elderly patients (Zhang et al., 2021). To assure the access and safeguard the appropriateness of safe, effective and quality medicines, the government, the Hospital Authority and the medical profession, together with the nurses and pharmacists, should collaborate to develop the right policies and clinical practice guidelines in steering better therapeutic decisions. It is also equally important to educate the elderly patients on the knowledge and handling of medications.

Coverage of vaccines in Hong Kong

Vaccination is also integral to universal health coverage. The annual seasonal influenza is a major disease burden in Hong Kong. The HKSAR government has launched the free Government Vaccination Programme for the elderly and people from 50 to 64 years of age currently on social security, and the Vaccination Subsidy Scheme, which provides subsidised seasonal influenza vaccination and pneumococcal vaccination to eligible Hong Kong residents by enrolled private doctors (Centre for Health Protection, 2021b). Local residents aged 50 or above and 65 or above are highly encouraged to receive the seasonal influenza vaccination and pneumococcal vaccination, respectively. The annual vaccination rate for community-dwelling elderly in Hong Kong had been very low. The unsatisfactory vaccination rate among the elderly was associated with the limited knowledge, limited public awareness and negative experience of vaccination (Mo & Lau, 2015; Sun et al., 2020; Wang et al., 2021; Yu et al., 2014). The vaccination rate increased to over 40% after 2018 due to public awareness about the benefits of vaccines and the subsidy scheme (Centre for Health Protection, 2021a; Sun et al., 2020; Wang et al., 2021; Yang et al., 2020). More works are needed to promote the vaccination programmes to the elderly and to strongly encourage them to get vaccinated to avoid influenza-related complications.

Vaccination is essential for the public health because it helps to minimise the spread of communicable diseases, thus relieving the pressure and demand on health services. Expenditure on vaccines is highly associated with vaccine coverage and improvement of health outcomes (Onishchenko et al., 2019). In Hong Kong, seasonal influenza vaccination and pneumococcal vaccination were promoted for the elderly every year. The quantities of seasonal influenza vaccination and pneumococcal vaccination were increased in the past several years (Department of Health, 2018b, 2021b). The estimated spending on seasonal influenza vaccination and pneumococcal vaccination in 2021/22 would be more than HK$176 million, an increase of around 21% than the previous year. During the COVID-19 pandemic, the HKSAR government has earmarked over HK$8.4 billion for the procurement and administration of COVID-19 vaccines (Chan, 2021). Hong Kong has excellent access and coverage of vaccines. This is more obvious among the elderly as a result of the policy and associated programmes by the HKSAR government.

References

Abdullah, A. S. M., Ho, L. M., Kwan, Y. H., Cheung, W. L., McGhee, S. M., & Chan, W. H. (2006). Promoting smoking cessation among the elderly: What are the predictors of intention to quit and successful quitting? *Journal of Aging and Health, 18*(4), 552–564. https://doi.org/10.1177%2F0898264305281104

Apollonio, D. E., Dutra, L. M., & Glantz, S. A. (2021). Associations between smoking trajectories, smoke-free laws and cigarette taxes in a longitudinal sample of youth and young adults. *PLoS One, 16*(2), e0246321. https://doi.org/10.1371/journal.pone.0246321

Bhatta, M., Nandi, S., Dutta, N., Dutta, S., & Saha, M. K. (2020). HIV care among elderly population: Systematic review and meta-analysis. *AIDS Research and Human Retroviruses, 36*(6), 475–489. https://doi.org/10.1089/aid.2019.0098

Census and Statistics Department. (2011). *Thematic household survey report no. 48: Pattern of smoking, keeping of dogs and cats, pattern of using non-franchised bus services, personal computer and internet penetration, environmental noise issues.* www.censtatd.gov.hk/en/data/stat_report/product/C0000047/att/B11302482011XXXXB0100.pdf

Census and Statistics Department. (2020a). *Hong Kong poverty situation report 2019.* www.censtatd.gov.hk/en/data/stat_report/product/B9XX0005/att/B9XX0005E2019AN19E0100.pdf

Census and Statistics Department. (2020b). *Thematic household survey report no. 70: Pattern of smoking.* www.censtatd.gov.hk/en/data/stat_report/product/C0000047/att/B11302702020XXXXB0100.pdf

Centre for Health Protection. (2017). *HIV infection.* www.chp.gov.hk/en/healthtopics/content/24/26.html

Centre for Health Protection. (2020a). *Number of deaths by leading causes of death by sex by age in 2019.* www.chp.gov.hk/en/statistics/data/10/27/340.html

Centre for Health Protection. (2020b). *Tuberculosis notifications (all forms) and rate by age group and sex, 2020 (Provisional).* www.chp.gov.hk/en/statistics/data/10/26/43/6942.html

Centre for Health Protection. (2021a). *Statistics on vaccination programmes in the past 3 years.* www.chp.gov.hk/en/features/102226.html

Centre for Health Protection. (2021b). *Vaccination Subsidy Scheme: General public.* www.chp.gov.hk/en/features/46107.html

Centre for Suicide Research and Prevention. (2020). *Suicide rates by age group in Hong Kong 1981–2019.* https://csrp.hku.hk/statistics/

Chan, F., Wu, J., Ng, S., Ng, S., Wong, M. C. S., & Ching, J. (2020). *Evaluation of the colorectal cancer screening pilot program in Hong Kong: Awareness, knowledge, attitude, perception, practice and satisfaction of stakeholders.* https://rfs1.fhb.gov.hk/search/#/fundedsearch/projectdetail?id=1904&lang=en

Chan, K., & Tsang, L. (2018). Public attitudes toward traditional Chinese medicine and how they affect medical treatment choices in Hong Kong. *International Journal of Pharmaceutical and Healthcare Marketing, 12*(2), 113–125. https://doi.org/10.1108/IJPHM-02-2017-0009

Chan, P. (2021). *The 2021–22 budget.* www.budget.gov.hk/2021/eng/pdf/e_budget_speech_2021-22.pdf

Chan-Yeung, M., Koo, L. C., Ho, J. M., Tsang, K. T., Chau, W. S., Chiu, S. W., Ip, M. M., & Lam, W. K. (2003). Risk factors associated with lung cancer in Hong Kong. *Lung Cancer*, *40*(2), 131–140. https://doi.org/10.1016/S0169-5002(03)00036-9

Chinese Medicine Development Fund. (2021). *Introduction*. www.cmdevfund.hk/content-en.php?mid=1

Chiu, H. F. K., Yip, P. S. F., Chi, I., Chan, S., Tsoh, J., Kwan, C. W., Li, S. F., Conwell, Y., & Caine, E. (2004). Elderly suicide in Hong Kong: A case-controlled psychological autopsy study. *Acta Psychiatrica Scandinavica*, *109*(4), 299–305. https://doi.org/10.1046/j.1600-0447.2003.00263.x

Chong, K. C., Leung, C. C., Yew, W. W., Zee, B. C. Y., Tam, G. C. H., Wang, M. H., . . . Yeoh, E. K. (2019). Mathematical modelling of the impact of treating latent tuberculosis infection in the elderly in a city with intermediate tuberculosis burden. *Scientific Reports*, *9*(1), 1–11. https://doi.org/10.1038/s41598-019-41256-4

Chung, R. Y. N., Chan, D., Chau, N. N. S., Huang, S., Wong, H., & Wong, S. Y. S. (2019). Poverty affects access to regular source of primary care among the general population in Hong Kong. *Social Policy & Administration*, *53*(6), 854–871. https://doi.org/10.1111/spol.12538

Cobiac, L. J., Ikeda, T., Nghiem, N., Blakely, T., & Wilson, N. (2015). Modelling the implications of regular increases in tobacco taxation in the tobacco endgame. *Tobacco Control*, *24*(e2), e154–e160. https://doi.org/10.1136/tobaccocontrol-2014-051543

Department of Health. (2008). *Promoting health in Hong Kong: A strategic framework for prevention and control of non-communicable diseases*. www.change4health.gov.hk/filemanager/common/image/strategic_framework/promoting_health/promoting_health_e.pdf

Department of Health. (2017). *Report of population health survey 2014/2015*. www.chp.gov.hk/files/pdf/dh_phs_2014_15_full_report_eng.pdf

Department of Health. (2018a). *Acting on non-communicable diseases*. www.chp.gov.hk/files/pdf/ncd_watch_may_2018.pdf

Department of Health. (2018b). *Replies in written questions raised by finance committee members in examining the estimates of expenditure 2018–19*. www.dh.gov.hk/english/budget/files/2018-19_eng.pdf

Department of Health. (2018c). *Towards 2025: Strategy and action plan to prevent and control non-communicable diseases in Hong Kong*. www.chp.gov.hk/files/pdf/saptowards2025_fullreport_en.pdf

Department of Health. (2019). *Guidelines on prevention of communicable diseases in residential care homes for the elderly*. www.chp.gov.hk/files/pdf/guidelines_on_prevention_of_communicable_diseases_in_rche_eng.pdf

Department of Health. (2021a). *HIV surveillance report: 2019 update*. www.chp.gov.hk/files/pdf/aids19.pdf

Department of Health. (2021b). *Replies in written questions raised by finance committee members in examining the estimates of expenditure 2021–22*. www.dh.gov.hk/english/budget/files/2021-22_eng.pdf

Drug Office. (2014). *Oral antituberculosis drugs*. www.drugoffice.gov.hk/eps/do/en/consumer/news_informations/dm_32.html#a

Flores-Flores, O., Bell, R., Reynolds, R., & Bernabé-Ortiz, A. (2018). Older adults with disability in extreme poverty in Peru: How is their access to health care? *PLoS One, 13*(12), e0208441. https://doi.org/10.1371/journal.pone.0208441

Fong, B. Y., Wong, M., Law, V. T., Lo, M. F., Ng, T. K., Yee, H. H., . . . Ho, P. W. (2020). Relationships between physical and social behavioural changes and the mental status of homebound residents in Hong Kong during the COVID-19 pandemic. *International Journal of Environmental Research and Public Health, 17*(18), 6653. https://doi.org/10.3390/ijerph17186653

Food and Health Bureau. (2017). *Mental health review report.* www.fhb.gov.hk/download/press_and_publications/otherinfo/180500_mhr/e_mhr_full_report.pdf

Food and Health Bureau. (2018). *Hong Kong reference framework for diabetes care for adults in primary care settings.* www.fhb.gov.hk/pho/rfs/english/reference_framework/diabetes_care.html

Food and Health Bureau. (2021). *Hong Kong's domestic health accounts (DHA).* www.fhb.gov.hk/statistics/download/dha/en/a_estimate_1920.pdf

Fu, Y. Y., Chui, E. W. T., Law, C. K., Zhao, X., & Lou, V. W. (2018). An exploration of older Hong Kong residents' willingness to make copayments toward vouchers for community care. *Journal of Aging & Social Policy, 31*(4), 358–377. https://doi.org/10.1080/08959420.2018.1467157

Fujita, M., Sato, Y., Nagashima, K., Takahashi, S., & Hata, A. (2016). Income related inequality of health care access in Japan: A retrospective cohort study. *PLoS One, 11*(3), e0151690. https://doi.org/10.1371/journal.pone.0151690

Fung, V. L. H., Lai, A. H. Y., Yam, C. H. K., Wong, E. L. Y., Griffiths, S. M., & Yeoh, E. K. (2020). Healthcare vouchers for better elderly services? Input from private healthcare service providers in Hong Kong. *Health & Social Care in the Community,* 1–13. https://doi.org/10.1111/hsc.13203

The Government of the Hong Kong Special Administrative Region. (2021). *Government launches Phase 1 of mental health initiatives funding scheme.* www.info.gov.hk/gia/general/202107/30/P2021073000317.htm

Harding, E. (2020). WHO global progress report on tuberculosis elimination. *The Lancet Respiratory Medicine, 8*(1), 19. https://doi.org/10.1016/S2213-2600(19)30418-7

Health Care Voucher. (2021). *Types of healthcare service providers.* www.hcv.gov.hk/en/hcvs/target_group.html

Hong Kong Advisory Council on AIDS. (2016). *Report of the community stakeholders' consultation for the development of recommended HIV/AIDS strategies for Hong Kong.* www.aca.gov.hk/english/strategies/pdf/csc17-21.pdf

Hong Kong AIDS Foundation. (2018). *Support services for people living with HIV (PLHIV).* www.aids.org.hk/?page_id=1535

Hong Kong Cancer Registry. (2020). *Overview of Hong Kong cancer statistics of 2018.* https://www3.ha.org.hk/cancereg/pdf/overview/Overview%20of%20HK%20Cancer%20Stat%202018.pdf

Hong Kong Cancer Registry. (2021). *Cancer statistics query systems.* https://www3.ha.org.hk/cancereg/allages.asp

Hong Kong Council on Smoking and Health. (2021a). *Elderly smoking cessation promotion project.* https://smokefree.hk/page.php?id=20&lang=en

Hong Kong Council on Smoking and Health. (2021b). *Tobacco tax*. www.smokefree. hk/page.php?id=91&lang=en

Hong Kong Family Welfare Society. (2021). *Community care and support services for the elderly*. www.hkfws.org.hk/en/how-we-help/elderly-and-community-support-services/elderly-mental-health

Hong Kong Tuberculosis, Chest and Heart Diseases Association. (2021). *History*. https://antitb.org.hk/en/about_us.php?cid=1

Hospital Authority. (2021). *Major statistics*. https://www3.ha.org.hk/Data/HAStatistics/MajorReport

Huang, J., Wang, J., Pang, T. W. Y., Chan, M. K. Y., Leung, S., Chen, X., Leung, C., Zheng, Z. J., & Wong, M. C. S. (2020). Does theory of planned behaviour play a role in predicting uptake of colorectal cancer screening? A cross-sectional study in Hong Kong. *BMJ Open, 10*(8), e037619. https://doi.org/10.1136/bmjopen-2020-037619

Hung, K., Bai, X., & Lu, J. (2016). Understanding travel constraints among the elderly in Hong Kong: A comparative study of the elderly living in private and in public housing. *Journal of Travel & Tourism Marketing, 33*(7), 1051–1070. https://doi.org/10.1080/10548408.2015.1084975

Jarzebski, M. P., Elmqvist, T., Gasparatos, A., Fukushi, K., Eckersten, S., Haase, D., . . . Pu, J. (2021). Ageing and population shrinking: Implications for sustainability in the urban century. *NPJ Urban Sustainability, 1*(1), 1–11. https://doi.org/10.1038/s42949-021-00023-z

Joseph, A. M., Rothman, A. J., Almirall, D., Begnaud, A., Chiles, C., Cinciripini, P. M., Fu, S. S., Graham, A. L., Lindgren, B. R., Melzer, A. C., Ostrof, J. S., Seaman, E. L., Taylor, K. L., Toll, B. A., Zeliadt, S. B., & Vock, D. M. (2018). Lung cancer screening and smoking cessation clinical trials. SCALE (smoking cessation within the context of lung cancer screening) collaboration. *American Journal of Respiratory and Critical Care Medicine, 197*(2), 172–182. https://doi.org/10.1164/rccm.201705-0909CI

Kwong, E., Kwok, T. T., Sumerlin, T. S., Goggins, W. B., Leung, J., & Kim, J. H. (2020). Does subjective social status predict depressive symptoms in Chinese elderly? A longitudinal study from Hong Kong. *Journal of Epidemiology and Community Health, 74*(11), 882–891. https:// doi.org/10.1136/jech-2019-212451

Lai, A. H. Y., Kuang, Z., Yam, C. H. K., Ayub, S., & Yeoh, E. K. (2017). Vouchers for primary healthcare services in an ageing world? The perspectives of elderly voucher recipients in Hong Kong. *Health & Social Care in the Community, 26*(3), 374–382. https://doi.org/10.1111/hsc.12523

Lam, G. (2020). Problems encountered by elders in residential care services in Hong Kong. *Asian Education and Development Studies*. https://doi.org/10.1108/AEDS-09-2019-0158

Lau, B. H., Chan, C. L., & Ng, S. M. (2021). Resilience of Hong Kong people in the COVID-19 pandemic: Lessons learned from a survey at the peak of the pandemic in Spring 2020. *Asia Pacific Journal of Social Work and Development, 31*(1–2), 105–114. https://doi.org/10.1080/02185385.2020.1778516

Lee, D. T., Yu, D., Ip, M., & Tang, J. Y. (2017). Evaluation on the implementation of respiratory protection measures in old age homes. *Clinical Interventions in Aging, 12*, 1429. https://doi.org/10.2147/CIA.S142522

Lee, S. Y., & Chou, K. L. (2016). Trends in elderly poverty in Hong Kong: A decomposition analysis. *Social Indicators Research, 129*(2), 551–564. https://doi.org/10.1007/s11205-015-1120-5

Lee, S. Y., & Chou, K. L. (2019). Assessing the relative contribution of social exclusion, income-poverty, and financial strain on depressive symptoms among older people in Hong Kong. *Aging & Mental Health, 23*(11), 1487–1495. https://doi.org/10.1080/13607863.2018.1506740

Legislative Council Secretariat. (2017). *Residential care services for the elderly.* www.legco.gov.hk/research-publications/english/1617issh22-residential-care-services-for-the-elderly-20170314-e.pdf

Legislative Council Secretariat. (2019). *Hospital Authority drug formulary.* www.legco.gov.hk/research-publications/english/1819issh35-hospital-authority-drug-formulary-20191002-e.pdf

Legislative Council Secretariat. (2020). *Preventive healthcare services.* www.legco.gov.hk/research-publications/english/1920issh30-preventive-healthcare-services-20200630-e.pdf

Legislative Council Secretariat. (2021). *Community care services for the elderly in Germany and Japan.* www.legco.gov.hk/research-publications/english/2021in12-community-care-services-for-the-elderly-in-germany-and-japan-20210616-e.pdf

Li, W., Tse, L. A., Au, J. S., Wang, F., Qiu, H., & Yu, I. T. S. (2016). Secondhand smoke enhances lung cancer risk in male smokers: An interaction. *Nicotine & Tobacco Research, 18*(11), 2057–2064. https://doi.org/10.1093/ntr/ntw115

Lian, J., McGhee, S. M., So, C., Chau, J., Wong, C. K., Wong, W. C., & Lam, C. L. (2017). Five-year cost-effectiveness of the Patient Empowerment Programme (PEP) for type 2 diabetes mellitus in primary care. *Diabetes, Obesity and Metabolism, 19*(9), 1312–1316. https://doi.org/10.1111/dom.12919

Mo, P. K. H., & Lau, J. T. F. (2015). Influenza vaccination uptake and associated factors among elderly population in Hong Kong: The application of the health belief model. *Health Education Research, 30*(5), 706–718. https://doi.org/10.1093/her/cyv038

Ng, S. C., & Wong, S. H. (2013). Colorectal cancer screening in Asia. *British Medical Bulletin, 105*(1), 29–42. https://doi.org/10.1093/bmb/lds040

Onishchenko, K., Hill, S., Wasserman, M., Jones, C., Moffatt, M., Ruff, L., & Pugh, S. J. (2019). Trends in vaccine investment in middle income countries. *Human Vaccines & Immunotherapeutics, 15*(10), 2378–2385. https://doi.org/10.1080/21645515.2019.1589287

Panel on Health Services. (2021). *Updated background brief prepared by the Legislative Council Secretariat.* www.legco.gov.hk/yr20-21/english/panels/hs/papers/hs20210514cb4-973-6-e.pdf

Peters, D. H., Garg, A., Bloom, G., Walker, D. G., Brieger, W. R., & Hafizur Rahman, M. (2008). Poverty and access to health care in developing countries. *Annals of the New York Academy of Sciences, 1136*(1), 161–171. https://doi.org/10.1196/annals.1425.011

Qiu, D., Chen, T., Liu, T., & Song, F. (2020). Smoking cessation and related factors in middle-aged and older Chinese adults: Evidence from a longitudinal study. *PLoS One, 15*(10), e0240806. https://doi.org/10.1371/journal.pone.0240806

Research Fund Secretariat. (2021). *About HMRF.* https://rfs1.fhb.gov.hk/english/funds/funds_hmrf/funds_hmrf_abt/funds_hmrf_abt.html

Sau Po Centre on Ageing. (2019). *A survey of elderly mental health in Hong Kong: Final report 2019.* https://ageing.hku.hk/upload/file/elderly_mental_health_report-s.pdf

Sheng, L., Tu, J. W., Tian, J. H., Chen, H. J., Pan, C. L., & Zhou, R. Z. (2018). A meta-analysis of the relationship between environmental tobacco smoke and lung cancer risk of nonsmoker in China. *Medicine, 97*(28). https://doi.org/10.1097/MD.0000000000011389

Statistics of Japan. (2021). *Vital statistics.* www.e-stat.go.jp/en/stat-search/files?page=1&toukei=00450011&tstat=000001028897

Sun, K. S., Cheng, Y. H., Wun, Y. T., & Lam, T. P. (2017). Choices between Chinese and Western medicine in Hong Kong–interactions of institutional environment, health beliefs and treatment outcomes. *Complementary Therapies in Clinical Practice, 28,* 70–74. https://doi.org/10.1016/j.ctcp.2017.05.012

Sun, K. S., Lam, T. P., Kwok, K. W., Lam, K. F., Wu, D., & Ho, P. L. (2020). Seasonal influenza vaccine uptake among Chinese in Hong Kong: Barriers, enablers and vaccination rates. *Human Vaccines & Immunotherapeutics, 16*(7), 1675–1684. https://doi.org/10.1080/21645515.2019.1709351

Sun, W. J., Xu, L., Chan, W. M., Lam, T. H., & Schooling, C. M. (2012). Depressive symptoms and suicide in 56,000 older Chinese: A Hong Kong cohort study. *Social Psychiatry and Psychiatric Epidemiology, 47*(4), 505–514. https://doi.org/10.1007/s00127-011-0362-z

Tam, G., Yang, H., & Meyers, T. (2018). Mixed methods study on elimination of tuberculosis in Hong Kong. *Hong Kong Medical Journal, 24*(4), 400–407. https://doi.org/10.12809/hkmj177141

Tobacco and Alcohol Control Office. (2021). *Tobacco control legislation.* www.taco.gov.hk/t/english/legislation/legislation_sa.html

Tse, L. A., Lin, X., Li, W., Qiu, H., Chan, C. K., Wang, F., . . . Leung, C. C. (2018). Smoking cessation sharply reduced lung cancer mortality in a historical cohort of 3185 Chinese silicotic workers from 1981 to 2014. *British Journal of Cancer, 119*(12), 1557–1562. https://doi.org/10.1038/s41416-018-0292-6

Tse, L. A., Yu, I. T. S., Qiu, H., Au, J. S. K., Wang, X. R., Tam, W., & Yu, K. S. (2011). Lung cancer decreased sharply in first 5 years after smoking cessation in Chinese men. *Journal of Thoracic Oncology, 6*(10), 1670–1676. https://doi.org/10.1097/JTO.0b013e3182217bd4

Tso, I. F., & Park, S. (2020). Alarming levels of psychiatric symptoms and the role of loneliness during the COVID-19 epidemic: A case study of Hong Kong. *Psychiatry Research, 293,* 113423. https://doi.org/10.1016/j.psychres.2020.113423

United Nations Development Programme. (2020). *Human development report 2020.* http://hdr.undp.org/sites/default/files/hdr2020.pdf

Verguet, S., Tarr, G., Gauvreau, C. L., Mishra, S., Jha, P., Liu, L., Xiao, Y., Qiu, Y., & Zhao, K. (2017). Distributional benefits of tobacco tax and smoke–free workplaces in China: A modeling study. *Journal of Global Health, 7*(2). https:/doi.org/10.7189/jogh.07.020701

Virtual AIDS Office of Hong Kong. (2021a). *About us.* www.aids.gov.hk/english/main.html

Virtual AIDS Office of Hong Kong. (2021b). *Review of HIV/AIDS in first quarter of 2021.* www.aids.gov.hk/english/

Wang, Z., Fang, Y., Ip, M., Lau, M., & Lau, J. T. (2021). Facilitators and barriers to completing recommended doses of pneumococcal vaccination among community-living individuals aged ≥ 65 years in Hong Kong: A population-based study. *Human Vaccines & Immunotherapeutics, 17*(2), 527–536. https://doi.org/1 0.1080/21645515.2020.1776545

Wong, C. K. H., Lam, C. L., Wan, E. Y., Chan, A. K., Pak, C. H., Chan, F. W., & Wong, W. C. (2016a). Evaluation of patient-reported outcomes data in structured diabetes education intervention: 2-year follow-up data of patient empowermentprogramme.*Endocrine,54*(2),422–432.https://doi.org/10.1007/s12020-016-1015-5

Wong, C. K. H., Wong, W. C. W., Wan, Y. F., Chan, A. K. C., Chan, F. W. K., & Lam, C. L. K. (2016b). Effect of a structured diabetes education programme in primary care on hospitalizations and emergency department visits among people with type 2 diabetes mellitus: Results from the Patient Empowerment Programme. *Diabetic Medicine, 33*(10), 1427–1436. https://doi.org/10.1111/dme.12969

Wong, G. C., Ng, T., & Li, T. (2019). Infection control in residential care homes for the elderly in Hong Kong (2005–2014). *Hong Kong Medical Journal, 25*(2), 113–119. https://doi.org/10.12809/hkmj187328

Wong, M. C., Wang, H. H., Kwan, M. W., Chan, W. M., Fan, C. K., Liang, M., Li, S. T., Fung, F. D., Yeung, M. S., Chan, D. K., & Griffiths, S. M. (2016c). The adoption of the Reference Framework for diabetes care among primary care physicians in primary care settings: A cross-sectional study. *Medicine, 95*(31). https://doi.org/10.1097/MD.0000000000004108

Wong, S. Y. S., Zhang, D., Sit, R. W. S., Yip, B. H. K., Chung, R. Y. N., Wong, C. K. M., Chan, D. C. C., Sun, W., Kwok, K. O., & Mercer, S. W. (2020). Impact of COVID-19 on loneliness, mental health, and health service utilisation: A prospective cohort study of older adults with multimorbidity in primary care. *British Journal of General Practice, 70*(700), e817–e824. https://doi.org/10.3399/bjgp20X713021

World Health Organization. (2021). *Older people & COVID-19.* www.who.int/teams/social-determinants-of-health/demographic-change-and-healthy-ageing/covid-19

Yang, L., Hu, W. B., Wong, C. M., Chiu, S. S. S., Soares Magalhaes, R. J., Thach, T. Q., Clements, A. C. A., & Peiris, J. S. M. (2020). Effect of increased influenza and pneumococcal vaccine coverage on the burden of influenza among elderly people in Hong Kong versus Brisbane: Abridged secondary publication. *Hong Kong Medical Journal, 4*(3), 12–16.

Yu, D. S. F., Low, L. P. L., Lee, I. F. K., Lee, D. T. F., & Ng, W. M. (2014). Predicting influenza vaccination intent among at-risk Chinese older adults in Hong Kong. *Nursing Research, 63*(4), 270–277. https://doi.org/10.1097/NNR.0000000000000028

Yu, R., Leung, J., Lum, C. M., Auyeung, T. W., Lee, J. S., Lee, R., & Woo, J. (2019). A comparison of health expectancies over 10 years: Implications for elderly service needs in Hong Kong. *International Journal of Public Health, 64*(5), 731–742. https://doi.org/10.1007/s00038-019-01240-1

Zhang, H., Wong, E. L., Yeoh, E. K., & Ma, B. H. (2021). Development of an explicit tool assessing potentially inappropriate medication use in Hong Kong elder patients. *BMC Geriatrics*, *21*(1), 1–12. https://doi.org/10.1186/s12877-021-02024-0

Zhao, S. Z., Wong, J. Y. H., Luk, T. T., Wai, A. K. C., Lam, T. H., & Wang, M. P. (2020). Mental health crisis under COVID-19 pandemic in Hong Kong, China. *International Journal of Infectious Diseases*, *100*, 431–433. https://doi.org/10.1016/j.ijid.2020.09.030

3 Interconnectedness of Sustainable Development Goal 3 and Sustainable Development Goals related to ageing

Interconnectedness of Sustainable Development Goals related to ageing

The ageing problem is perceived as a challenging obstacle in achieving SDGs, such as the sustainability of labour markets economics and pension fund policies. The provision of health and welfare services is mostly discussed (Jarzebski et al., 2021). The relationship between health and ageing is inevitable, and SDG 3 is the main intersect between ageing and sustainability. Apart from putting more efforts in meeting the targets in SDG 3 to accomplish health improvement and quality of life, attention on other SDGs in relation to ageing is equally desirable because economic growth, social development and environmental protection are interdependent and mutually reinforcing components of sustainable development (Fonseca et al., 2020). The complex interactions between SDGs represent a challenge for governments and decision-makers across different countries. Poverty elimination (SDG 1) has a synergetic relationship with health and well-being (SDG 3), while sustainable cities and communities (SDG 11) also have interactive effects with SDG 3 (Fonseca et al., 2020). Ageing population poses even more barriers for countries to achieve SDGs as older people experience more challenges related to health, safety, capacity to deal with disasters, vulnerability to diseases/pandemics and mobility (Jarzebski et al., 2021). Opportunities and challenges in longer lives are heavily dependent on health, while many factors, such as financial security, housing, education and community safety, can also affect health. This chapter focuses on how SDG 1, SDG 4 and SDG 11 influence SDG 3 in relation to ageing in Hong Kong. Their interconnectedness with health and ageing will be discussed, and current policies and measures adopted in Hong Kong will be reviewed.

The related targets and relevant SDGs are listed as follows (United Nations, 2016):

DOI: 10.4324/9781003220169-3

Sustainable Development Goal 1 concerning older persons
SDG 1 No poverty

- Target 1.4: By 2030, ensure that all men and women, in particular the poor and the vulnerable, have equal rights to economic resources, as well as access to basic services, ownership and control over land and other forms of property, inheritance, natural resources, appropriate new technology and financial services, including microfinance

Sustainable Development Goal 4 concerning older persons
SDG 4 Quality education

- Target 4.3: By 2030, ensure equal access for all women and men to affordable and quality technical, vocational and tertiary education, including university
- Target 4.5: By 2030, eliminate gender disparities in education and ensure equal access to all levels of education and vocational training for the vulnerable, including persons with disabilities, indigenous peoples and children in vulnerable situations

Sustainable Development Goal 11 concerning older persons
SDG 11 Make cities and human settlements inclusive, safe, resilient and sustainable

- Target 11.1: By 2030, ensure access for all to adequate, safe and affordable housing and basic services and upgrade slums
- Target 11.2: By 2030, provide access to safe, affordable, accessible and sustainable transport systems for all, improving road safety, notably by expanding public transport, with special attention to the needs of those in vulnerable situations, women, children, persons with disabilities and older persons
- Target 11.3: By 2030, enhance inclusive and sustainable urbanisation and capacity for participatory, integrated and sustainable human settlement planning and management in all countries
- Target 11.7: By 2030, provide universal access to safe, inclusive and accessible, green and public spaces, in particular for women and children, older persons and persons with disabilities

Elimination of poverty to promote healthy ageing

To achieve healthy lives and promote well-being (SDG 3), eliminating poverty in any life stages, as suggested in SDG 1, is essential. Health inequalities arising from ethnicity, gender, age and socio-economic status (SES) have been widely researched in the literature. SES determines monthly household income, monthly household expenditure, education, occupation and housing tenure. These factors affect individual and household access to health and other social resources, such as food, housing and medical care (Brown et al., 2016). Prior studies have examined the effect of socio-economic status (SES) on health among older adults and found that their health will be worsened when economic disadvantage increases (Brown et al., 2016). The gradient relationship between SES and health is supported by evidence that the higher SES groups experience fewer health problems (Cai et al., 2017; Han et al., 2018; Ma & McGhee, 2013; Stolz et al., 2017; Wu & Wang, 2019). Furthermore, relating to occupational status and social resources, the level of education can change knowledge, problem solving skills, and awareness on health and self-management (Chen et al., 2014). People who have higher educational level would also have higher income during employment and, therefore, have a larger capacity to develop healthier lifestyles and health management in advanced age. Thus, they are comparatively healthier and have longer life expectancy (Hirai et al., 2012; Kim & Kim, 2016). This phenomenon has resulted in disparity in health among the elderly, and the health inequality situation is more obvious in less developed areas and rural communities where health resources and economic development are limited. As a consequence, elderly residents in rural areas are more prone to chronic conditions and frailty (Wu et al., 2018).

Among the SES indicators, income security is an important feature to all ages, as it affects the affordability to healthcare services and other basic necessities (Chung et al., 2020; Kyriopoulos et al., 2014). Older people tend to face a possible danger of either becoming or remaining poor because most of them are retired or have low participation in employment, making them at a greater risk of poverty (Lewis et al., 2020). Poverty status is a particular social determinant related to health, as poverty is found to be associated with increased level of frailty among elderly. Moreover, economic hardship has a strong association with their health-related quality of life (Chung et al., 2020; Ma & McGhee, 2013; Stolz et al., 2017). The reduction in income or reliance on personal saving, pension and social welfare constitutes a financial burden when covering out-of-pocket health expenditures and disease management (Yogo, 2016). In the community, there is a substantial fraction of elderly who are below the poverty line with pensions that are not enough to cover even the daily needs and even basic medical services (Jarzebski et al., 2021).

The poverty-health vicious cycle is illustrated by poor financial status through loss of income and increased susceptibility to healthcare costs or vice versa (Wagstaff, 2002). For example, older people tend to suffer from non-communicable diseases that require long-term care and increasingly expensive specialist healthcare services, and the financial consequences can exacerbate poverty (Chung et al., 2020; Muka et al., 2015). Furthermore, as most elderly people are retired, they do not normally use private healthcare services that are generally paid by out-of-pocket money or by medical insurance covered by employment (Chung et al., 2020). By the same reason, a healthier lifestyle is difficult to achieve among those elderly living in poverty if cheaper but less healthy food is consumed, leading to a greater risk in developing diseases (Chung et al., 2020). To break the poverty-health vicious cycle, the government must monitor the situation of poverty in the older population and formulate structural determinants with upstream policies to eliminate poverty (Chung et al, 2020; Woo et al., 2020).

Recurrent cash allowance

Poverty rate is regularly monitored in Hong Kong, and more than 1.4 million of the population were living in poverty in 2019. The poverty rate among older persons, aged 65 or above, increased by 1.1% from the preceding year to 32%. The total number of older persons suffering from poverty was around 391,200, which means almost four in every ten elderly persons lived in poverty (Census and Statistics Department, 2020a). The amount of direct financial assistance and other economic resources an older person receives can directly affect their ability to better manage healthcare expenditure and treatment. Therefore, the context of social welfare becomes a major factor that influences affordability. Through the poverty line set up by the Commission on Poverty (CoP), better resources have been allocated to assist in poverty alleviation among older persons. Being economically inactive, 85.7% of poor elders are receiving Comprehensive Social Security Assistance (CSSA), a welfare scheme for those who cannot support themselves financially. By helping more than 312,000 recipients at the end of September 2019, it is the most effective measure in tackling poverty (Census and Statistics Department, 2020a). The scheme includes Normal Disability Allowance, Higher Disability Allowance, Old Age Allowance, Normal Old Age Living Allowance, Higher Old Age Living Allowance, Guangdong Scheme and Fujian Scheme. Applicants of the Disability Allowance and Old Age Allowance under the scheme are not required to go through a means test (Social Welfare Department, 2021).

The Old Age Living Allowance (OALA) and Higher OALA were introduced in 2013 and 2018, respectively, to provide monthly allowance to support the living expenses of elderlies with financial needs (Census and Statistics Department, 2020a). OALA had alleviated the elderly poverty rate by 8.4% in 2019. A total of 592,900 OALA recipients were supported by the end of October 2020. In addition to the poverty framework, the HK$2 transport fare concession scheme was launched in 2012 to enable the elderly and disabled people to use public transport, such as the mass transit rail (MTR), franchised buses, minibuses and ferries with just HK$2 per trip irrespective of the distance (Labour and Welfare Bureau, 2021). With effect from 2022, the scheme would also benefit residents from the age of 60. The scheme does not only subsidise the older people in transportation expenses but also encourage them to go out to meet their friends and family members, and be integrated and connected to the wider community.

Healthcare subsidy for the elderly

Well-established healthcare protection for older persons surely facilitates effective prevention and control of diseases for this group and the community. In the context of healthcare policy, the HKSAR government has pledged to provide lifelong holistic health care to every citizen and to ensure that no one is denied adequate medical treatment due to lack of means. Older persons can use all high-quality and equitable health services. Public hospitals under the Hospital Authority (HA) and services of the Department of Health are heavily subsidised. An elderly can have access to the general outpatient clinics and other publicly funded health services and centres. In addition, there are some financial subsidies provided to the vulnerable group including the elderly. For instance, the policy of Waiving of Medical Charges ensures that the elderly will receive the health care despite financial difficulty. Recipients of CSSA and OALA aged 75 or above will be waived from payment of public medical fees (Hospital Authority, 2021). Voucher holders of the Pilot Scheme on Residential Care Service Voucher for the Elderly, a scheme that provides subsidised residential care to elderly persons, enjoy the waiving of payment of public medical fees up to HK$168,000. The waiving also covers low-income groups, chronical ill patients and elderly people who have little income or assets, subject to the means test of eligibility on financial criteria. Furthermore, the Elderly Health Care Voucher Scheme mentioned in the last chapter also helps in alleviating poverty among the elderly. The annual voucher amount of HK$2,000 can subsidise elderly people's primary healthcare services and ease their financial burden. The payment-waiving policy implemented by the HKSAR government is providing effective healthcare protection to the older population in the spirit of SDG 1, with respect to promoting equal rights to economic resources and access to basic services.

Education and health in the elderly

In Hong Kong and Singapore, 9.5% and 19.8% of elderlies, respectively, have at least secondary or higher education qualification or above (Census and Statistics Department, 2018; Department of Statistics, 2021).

Education level is associated with the score of healthy ageing, meaning low education level might have poor health conditions and outcomes (Wu et al., 2020). Similarly, higher education level is related to a higher health-related quality of life among the elderly (Kim et al., 2018). Promoting lifelong education opportunities for all is embedded in one of the sustainable development goals, namely SDG 4. Lifelong education is an important intervention to reduce the difference in education and pursue healthy ageing among the elderly, and is highly associated with quality of life (Leung & Liu, 2011; Ng et al., 2018a). Improving the accessibility and involvement in learning in later life can effectively improve health conditions (Mestheneos & Withnall, 2016). The significance of lifelong learning among elderly people could have major benefits, including maintaining cognitive functioning, enhancing social interaction with others and broadening social network, improving self-esteem and self-confidence, and improving quality of life (Tam, 2018).

There are various study options for adult learners in Hong Kong. For older adults, informal and formal learning are both available, but the options of formal studies offered by tertiary institutions are relatively limited. Lifelong learning programmes for the elderly are available in the forms of classroom learning, radio broadcasting and elder academy (Chui, 2012). A school-based Elder Academy Scheme was launched in 2007 to establish the Elder Academy, to promote lifelong learning and maintain good health among the elderly in Hong Kong (Chan & Liang, 2013). The elderly academy would be set up in primary, secondary and tertiary institutions with funding from the Elder Academy Scheme. About 180 elder academies, including 6 at the local universities, had been set up, providing more than 10,000 learning places. Courses offered included introduction to Chinese medicine, ink painting, information and communication technology, health, and other types of knowledge (Elder Academy, 2020). Nevertheless, funding for the elder academy was limited, and service providers were facing the dilemma of offering courses to address the wants of the elder learners, and entertain the needs of knowledge and skills in the long run (Tam, 2019). Moreover, there was limited information and inadequate evaluation about the effectiveness of the Elder Academy Scheme.

The government and NGOs provide different informal learning courses for the elderly. The Leisure and Cultural Service Department of the HKSAR government regularly provide a number of various courses, such as fitness and swimming training classes, tai chi classes, general gymnastics and other training courses for the elderly. Most of these courses are free of charge and are attractive to the elderly. However, the quota for each course is very limited. Places are allocated by balloting, and thus, most elderly people cannot join the course regularly. In practice, all the courses are inadequate to cater for the ageing population due to the limited quota in each course.

To promote lifelong learning in the society, the HKSAR government had set up the Continuing Education Fund to subsidise each citizen aged 18 to 70 in pursuing continuing education and training to a maximum amount of HK$20,000 (Continuing Education Fund, 2019). Eligible citizens are reimbursed for the fees of courses, which have been approved by the Continuing Education Fund. However, elderlies aged 71 or above are not included in the subsidy scheme of the Continuing Education Fund. This is a gross inadequacy of the inclusive policy and requires the attention and due consideration of the government, policymakers and educators. The upper age limit must be lifted, as the arrangement is discriminating against citizens who continue to live longer and are active in learning.

To encourage the elderly to continue lifelong learning, it is important to understand the needs of this age group. Tam and Chui (2015) show more than half of the older adults had rated learning in their later life as fairly important in Hong Kong. They preferred to continue lifelong learning because they wished to avoid degeneration of the body, understand their own health conditions and cope with the loss of a job or partner (Boulton-Lewis et al., 2016; Boulton-Lewis et al., 2017). They also liked to learn something that was useful in their daily lives or for leisure and interest (Tam, 2016). New knowledge related to health conditions combined with leisure generated from attending the courses are keeping the elderly people's desire to learn in their later life. With the enhanced knowledge of dementia, experiences in positive changes in psychological and social health were found in an elder learning course in Hong Kong (Yee et al., 2021). Conversely, there are some negative factors that may hinder lifelong learning, such as health conditions of the individual and family members, affordability of course fees and perception of being too old to learn (Tam, 2016). More studies and innovative strategies are needed to further develop education for the elderly as a Sustainable Development Goal.

Building a sustainable city and community for health status

Goal 11 aims to make cities and human settlements inclusive, safe, resilient and sustainable. An ageing population has an increased demand on the accessibility to safe public resources; for example, transportation, space and housing. There is a close relationship between SDG 11 and 3, as health outcomes are affected by urban policies in a sustainable and safe city. It is said that "health is a precondition of a sustainable city, through access to decent housing, clean air and water, nutritious food, safe transport and mobility, opportunities for physical activity, and protection from injury risks and toxic pollutants" (Ramirez-Rubio et al., 2019, p. 16). A good urban planning can reduce burdens of infectious and non-communicable diseases, thus improving health equity and enhancing well-being. For example, reducing adverse environmental effects and improving air quality will reduce cardiovascular and chronic respiratory diseases (Nugent et al., 2018). Effective transportation system, open spaces and water recycling system can help to prevent the concentration of polluted air and eliminate water and soil contamination (Ramirez-Rubio et al., 2019). In addition, Wong et al. (2017a) had shown that neighbourhood characteristics and domains of an age-friendly city, such as outdoor spaces, transportation and housing, were significantly associated with self-rated health. Furthermore, Fan (2020) discussed that a smart hospital (a key strategy of Hospital Authority) could improve the healthcare services efficiency in which patients and their families could benefit from this initiative.

Affordable housing and living environment

Housing is an important issue that is needed to be addressed in relation to the older population, as they spend comparatively more time at home than the other age groups or are even homebound, making housing an indispensable component of an age-friendly city (Jarzebski et al., 2021). Housing is the primary support of the welfare of all households and is one of the key issues in social and welfare policies of all governments (Ghaedrhmati & Shahsavari, 2019). It is a basic need and dwelling for the elderly to maintain security and comfort, as well as to benefit their physical and psychological health. The living environment, together with financial adequacy, physical safety and leisure activities, affects a person's living standards and quality of life (Leung et al., 2016). Poor housing, mostly due to affordability issues, can put an elderly at higher risk of injury, stress and isolation (World Health Organization, 2018). Subdivided houses or flats would have become their place of residence if they could not afford the rental. The poor environment affects the quality of life and individual mental well-being, leading to anxiety, depression and, possibly, hostility (Feng et al., 2018; Ng, 2019; Schneider-Skalska, 2019). Environmental and health risks are also associated with fire and disease outbreaks, and chronic issues caused by poor indoor air quality (Lam et al., 2021; Ng, 2019). Besides, architectural design of the residential buildings and facilities should be elderly friendly or age-friendly in order to fulfil the physical, psychological and social needs of the elderly (Leung et al., 2016; Ng et al., 2018b).

The housing problem in Hong Kong is getting more apparent with the increasing ageing population. Hong Kong, with limited living space to accommodate the high-density population, is also a city with a high living cost. Ranking at the bottom among 92 major housing markets in the world, the middle-income housing affordability rating in Hong Kong was 20.7 in 2020, representing a severely unaffordable level (Urban Reform Institute, 2021). Notably, half of the property rentals in Hong Kong cost more than HK$18,000 a month (Liu & Lam, 2018). Being in retirement and having a reduced income, expensive housing rentals cause stress and anxiety among the elderly. Increasing number of elderlies are staying in public housing due to their low-income status and reliance on life savings. Some of the more affluent elderlies live in private residence with poor living conditions, in very small, subdivided units of substandard living environment and high risk of safety, hygiene and other hazards, such as fire, water leakage and electrical leakage at home (Hui et al., 2014; Jayantha & Abeydeera, 2019). It is a challenge to the government in terms of proper and sufficient housing supply and affordable houses, particularly for the elderly and the vulnerable and underprivileged groups, such as the new migrants, ethnic minorities and people with disabilities (Leung et al., 2016).

There are a series of measures to respond in favour of the housing needs of the elderly under the concept of "housing for all" since 1998. The Hong Kong Housing Authority (HKHA) and the Hong Kong Housing Society (HKHS) offer various types of priority schemes for public rental housing (PRH) and rental allowance. The policy of the home-ownership scheme (HOS) plays an important role in the property market across the public and private section. Residents in public housing can purchase a private home at a 30% discount from the market price under the HOS. This arrangement allows these residents the opportunity not only to own their homes but also to vacate their public homes for those on the long waiting queue. Home ownership has become a priority option for older persons who desire better living quality (Hui et al., 2014). On the other hand, single elderlies can apply for Single Elderly Persons Priority Scheme, while families with two or more elderly persons can apply for the Harmonious Families Priority Scheme, which encourages the young generation to live with and take care of their parents or grandparents (Hong Kong Housing Authority, 2019). Importantly, the Rent Assistance Scheme (RAS) grants help for eligible applicants to reduce either 25% or 50% from the rental of PRH to provide financial relief (Hong Kong Housing Society, 2021a).

For the middle-income elderly, the Senior Citizen Residences Scheme (SEN) adopts an innovative "life-lease" approach, with a mixed model of retirement and assisted living (Hui et al., 2014). The scheme provides purpose-designed residence, integrating housing, recreation and medical care, to the elderly. Elderlies who are more financially capable can apply for a home in the non-subsidised senior housing project called "Tanner Hill Project", which is comprised of 590 independent living units with elderly friendly facilities and supporting features (Information Services Department, 2018).

In particular, the HKHS launched the Ageing-in-Place Scheme in 2012 to improve the living environment and quality of life of residents at aged 60 or above in the HKHS rental housing (Hong Kong Housing Society, 2021b). Twenty rental estates were involved in this scheme, which served more than 80,000 elderly people (Lam & Fong, 2020). Five domains of services were implemented in the scheme, including home safety, healthiness, autonomy, happiness and abled brain, to promote well-being, promote resilience to health decline and avoid premature institutionalisation. A longitudinal study on the Ageing-in-Place Scheme conducted in 2014–2018 found that the scheme successfully reduced the intention for institutional care, depressive symptoms, fall cases, and accidents and emergency services (Hong Kong Housing Society, 2021b). There were also increased satisfaction of the living environment and participation in community activities (Hong Kong Housing Society, 2021b).

Physical function of the elderly decreases with advancing age, resulting in increased incidence of falls. At the same time, elderly people need a safe environment to maintain physical exercises and carry out daily activities independently. The government has promoted age-friendly housing planning to improve the living environment of the elderly. The HKHA has adopted a universal design in all common areas of newly built public rental housing estates and units to create an age-friendly environment to cater to the elderly and persons with disabilities (Information Services Department, 2018). The universal design has included widened building entrances, corridors and doors to the flats to provide space for wheelchair users. The convenient and safer facilities will let the elderly and persons with disabilities live in the original unit continuously in their life so that they do not need to move to a new place when they get old (The Government of the Hong Kong Special Administrative Region, 2016). These government-led schemes comply with targets 11.3 and 11.7 of integrated and sustainable human settlement planning and management, and provide universal access to safe, inclusive and accessible green and public spaces, in particular for women and children, older persons, and persons with disabilities.

Accessible, safe and sustainable transportation

Inefficient transportation system is one of the biggest obstacles for sustainable development (Aguiar & Macário, 2017). Urban development to support ageing has been promoted by the World Health Organization. Access to transportation and outdoor places are key components in the development of an age-friendly city (Srichuae et al., 2016). Transportation refers to the movement of people or goods from one place to another. The ability to move around by taking public transport allows older people to independently engage in outdoor activities for attaining healthy ageing (Patil et al., 2020; Srichuae et al., 2016). Accessible and affordable public transportation is a key feature impelling active ageing, for instance, by accessing healthcare services in the community and other health-promoting activities and services, such as employment, shopping and social events, including visiting family, relatives and friends (Solomon et al., 2020). Expenditure on transportation may be a financial burden and affect the willingness to travel for the majority of the elderly, as they are retired and do not have any incentive or income for unnecessary expenses (Yuen, 2016). Other important factors that affect older adults with reducing mobility to access safe public transport include the availability of appropriate physical infrastructures, such as pedestrian pathways, proper seating arrangement in private and public areas, shelters, and disabled-friendly ramps (Aguiar & Macário, 2017; Cinderby et al., 2018). Furthermore, traffic-related air and noise pollution can directly affect the body and cause respiratory and cardiovascular health problems, as well as increase the risk of breast and prostate cancer (Lam et al., 2021; Widener & Hatzopoulou, 2016). Traffic congestion increases the emission of greenhouse gases, such as carbon dioxide and suspended particulates, leading to the heat island effect. These problems affect the health of the elderly and nearby residents.

Regarded as the one of the world's most successful and sophisticated transport network, Hong Kong has a well-developed and reliable public transportation system. The government has improved elderly people's mobility by increasing public transport share, which has become the major mode of transport with high transit usage (Wong et al., 2017b). It is estimated that there are 12.7 million passenger trips made by public transport each day and the MTR railway accounts for more than 40% (Burdett, 2019; Planning Department, 2016). Making MTR a backbone in transport services is an environmentally friendly and sustainable strategy, plus it serves a large capacity of passengers at any one time at affordable rates (Planning Department, 2016). With the opening of a new railway line, the Tuen Ma Line, and the construction of a bypass, the Central-Wan Chai Bypass, traffic congestion can be reduced and road safety can be improved. The Octopus payment method for all public transportation enables passengers to simply tap a card to the card reader at the point of entry or exit very conveniently. The HK$2 Transport Fare Scheme for the elderly and eligible persons with disabilities helps to encourage these groups to participate more in community and social activities. Extension of the scheme to include persons aged 60 to 64 in 2022 will benefit another 615,000 more people in the population (Research Office, 2021). Public transportation and the associated fare scheme will build a caring and inclusive society of Hong Kong.

However, elderly people are more prone to the risk of road traffic injuries (RTI) mainly due to their poor eyesight, musculoskeletal degeneration and slower reactions (Azami-Aghdash et al., 2018). A systematic review found that 23.5% elderly people were victims of RTI, which were mostly caused by bike accidents, car crashes and motorbike accidents (Azami-Aghdash et al., 2018). The casualty rate of people aged 60 or above increased to 2.8 per 1,000 population, while those aged 65 or above also increased to 2.3 per 1,000 population in 2018 (Census and Statistics Department, 2020b). The government plays an important role in the reduction of RTI by the implementation of prevention solutions, such as enhancing safety tools, like intelligent road cameras; regulating traffic rules, like preventing drunk driving; and promoting education on traffic safety (Azami-Aghdash, 2020). The Transport Department (TD) has introduced various pedestrian-friendly measures to add more walkability in urban areas. Helping to foster an age-friendly community, TD has applied the Octopus card technology in smart devices to extend the flashing green time for pedestrians. When the elderly or disabled persons cross the road at a pedestrian crossing, they can tap their Octopus card to activate the smart device to extend the flashing green time (Transport Department, 2021). Another measure was the introduction of priority seats in the public transport in 2009 for people in need, including the disabled, the elderly and pregnant ladies (Wong et al., 2017b).

Green and public open spaces

Many elderlies tend to spend more time in public open spaces after retirement. Public space and accessible green area improve air quality, reducing urban heat island effects and making urban environments more preferable (Gong et al., 2016). Previous studies have shown that green space is beneficial for human wellness through multiple pathways. For instance, access to and use of green space were recognised as factors that increased levels of physical health and recovery of mental illness among older people (Lau et al., 2021; Yu et al., 2018). In addition, Wang et al., (2017) found that higher coverage of green space was highly associated with reduced risks of all-cause mortality, circulatory system-caused mortality and stroke-caused mortality. Yu et al. (2018) showed that people who lived in places with higher percentage of green space was associated with improved frailty status. Fostering a successful retirement life and active ageing, exposure to green spaces facilitates the elderlies to enjoy leisure activities and socialise, thus enhancing their mental health and improving psychological state (Gong et al., 2016; Yu, 2021; Yung et al., 2016b). Generally, urban planners believe that better open space provision in urbanisation can improve social cohesion and promote a sense of belonging within the communities due to increased social interactions and less loneliness (Lam et al., 2021; Yu, 2021).

Hong Kong is a highly dense city and citizens usually live in small apartments or subdivided flats without gardens and backyards in Western countries. Open green spaces are, therefore, the primary venue to do various outdoor activities, including socialisation, backyard games and vegetable gardens (Lau et al., 2021). The common type of urban green spaces used in Hong Kong are green areas in public housing estates, street gardens and district parks (Lau et al., 2021). Green spaces in public housing estates are equipped with leisure and gymnastic facilities, while district parks, larger in size, are equipped with more public facilities, such as jogging tracks, public toilets and water features (Lau et al., 2021). Yung et al. (2016a) found out that "social and physical activities", "community life facilities and services", "social network" and "clean and pleasant environment" are the most important needs and factors in open spaces among older adults in Hong Kong. Instead of the quantity of open space area alone, Yu (2021) confirmed that community sense was influenced by the quality of open space, including the social and recreational facilities, locations and environment in Hong Kong.

More than 70% of the total land area of Hong Kong is covered by woodlands, shrublands and grasslands, making urban planning on green and open spaces rather challenging (The Government of the Hong Kong Special Administrative Region, 2019). The Hong Kong Planning Standards and Guidelines (HKPSG) provide a guidance for better urban design of greening and open space provision for citizens (Lau et al., 2021). There is still uneven distribution of public open spaces in the community. Some residents enjoy generous provisions, but others have less than the requirement in HKPSG of 2m² per person (Chow, 2018). Chow (2018) showed that approximately 93% of the population is within 400m of at least one type of public open spaces, such as parks and sports ground, but only 33% of residents can access large open spaces within 400m. Efforts have also been made to increase the number of small parks, gardens and sitting-out areas from 1,583 in 2020 to 1,648 in 2021 (Leisure and Cultural Services Department, 2021). Green spaces in public housing estates are managed by the HKHA, following the green design guideline. The HKHA has included 20% of the estate area and 30% of sites over two hectares for greening in all new estates (Lau et al., 2021).

The Urban Renewal Authority has provided about 26,000 square metres of open space in over 60 redevelopment projects. Urban redevelopment can improve the living environment with more greening and public open spaces and community facilities (Urban Renewal Authority, 2021). To utilise land resources more wisely, the "Hong Kong 2030+: Towards a Planning Vision and Strategy Transcending 2030" is a comprehensive strategic planning document on enhancing likeability with opportunities for recreation, leisure and culture (Development Bureau, 2016). One of the key directions of the plan is to adopt responsive urban design concepts, such as density differentials and open spaces. Catering to the changes in an ageing society in Hong Kong, the plan has proposed to promote age-friendly public space environment and adopt universal design in facilities.

References

Aguiar, B., & Macário, R. (2017). The need for an elderly centred mobility policy. *Transportation Research Procedia*, *25*, 4355–4369. https://doi.org/10.1016/j. trpro.2017.05.309

Azami-Aghdash, S. (2020). Meta-synthesis of qualitative evidence in road traffic injury prevention: A scoping review of qualitative studies (2000 to 2019). *Archives of Public Health*, *78*(1), 110. https://doi.org/10.1186/s13690-020-00493-0

Azami-Aghdash, S., Aghaei, M. H., & Sadeghi-Bazarghani, H. (2018). Epidemiology of road traffic injuries among elderly people: A systematic review and meta-Analysis. *Bulletin of Emergency and Trauma*, *6*(4), 279–291. https://doi. org/10.29252/beat-060403

Boulton-Lewis, G. M., Pike, L., Tam, M., & Buys, L. (2017). Ageing, loss, and learning: Hong Kong and Australian seniors. *Educational Gerontology*, *43*(2), 89–100. https://doi.org/10.1080/03601277.2016.1262144

Boulton-Lewis, G. M., Tam, M., Buys, L., & Chui, E. W. T. (2016). Hong Kong and Australian seniors: Views of aging and learning. *Educational Gerontology*, *42*(11), 758–770. https://doi.org/10.1080/03601277.2016.1231507

Brown, T. H., Richardson, L. J., Hargrove, T. W., & Thomas, C. S. (2016). Using multiple-hierarchy stratification and life course approaches to understand health inequalities: The intersecting consequences of race, gender, SES, and age. *Journal of Health and Social Behavior*, *57*(2), 200–222. https://doi.org/10.1177 %2F0022146516645165

Burdett, M. (2019). *Case study of transport infrastructure: Hong Kong*. www. geographycasestudy.com/case-study-of-transport-infrastructure-hong-kong/

Cai, J., Coyte, P. C., & Zhao, H. (2017). Determinants of and socio-economic disparities in self-rated health in China. *International Journal for Equity in Health*, *16*(1), 1–27. https://doi.org/10.1186/s12939-016-0496-4

Census and Statistics Department. (2018). *Hong Kong 2016 population by-census – Thematic report: Older persons.* www.censtatd.gov.hk/en/data/stat_report/product/ B1120105/att/B11201052016XXXXB0100.pdf

Census and Statistics Department. (2020a). *Hong Kong poverty situation report 2019*. www.povertyrelief.gov.hk/eng/pdf/Hong_Kong_Poverty_Situation_Report_2019.pdf

Census and Statistics Department. (2020b). *Road traffic accident statistics in Hong Kong, 2009 to 2018*. www.censtatd.gov.hk/en/data/stat_report/product/ FA100071/att/B72002FB2020XXXXB0100.pdf

Chan, C. M. A., & Liang, J. S. E. (2013). Active aging: Policy framework and applications to promote older adult participation in Hong Kong. *Ageing International*, *38*(1), 28–42. https://doi.org/10.1007/s12126-012-9166-z

Chen, C. X., Feng, L. N., & Li, S. X. (2014). The correlation between socioeconomic status and health self-management in the elderly. *International Journal of Nursing Sciences*, *1*(4), 410–415. https://doi.org/10.1016/j.ijnss.2014.10.008

Chow, J. (2018). *Public open space accessibility in Hong Kong*. https://civicexchange.org/wp-content/uploads/2018/10/Civic-Exchange-Public-Open-Space-Accessibility-in-Hong-Kong-GEOSPATIAL-ANALYSIS.pdf

Chui, E. (2012). Elderly learning in Chinese communities: China, Hong Kong, Taiwan and Singapore. In G. Boulton-Lewis & M. Tam (Eds.), *Active ageing, active learning: Education in the Asia-Pacific region: Issues, concerns and prospects* (pp. 141–162). Springer, Dordrecht. https://doi.org/10.1007/978-94-007-2111-1_9

Chung, G. K. K., Dong, D., Wong, S. Y. S., Wong, H., & Chung, R. Y. N. (2020). Perceived poverty and health, and their roles in the poverty-health vicious cycle: A qualitative study of major stakeholders in the healthcare setting in Hong Kong. *International Journal for Equity in Health*, *19*(1), 1–13. https://doi.org/10.1186/s12939-020-1127-7

Cinderby, S., Cambridge, H., Attuyer, K., Bevan, M., Croucher, K., Gilroy, R., & Swallow, D. (2018). Co-designing urban living solutions to improve older people's mobility and well-being. *Journal of Urban Health*, *95*(3), 409–422. https://doi.org/10.1007/s11524-018-0232-z

Continuing Education Fund. (2019). *Overview*. www.wfsfaa.gov.hk/cef/en/preparation/overview.htm

Department of Statistics. (2021). *Singapore census of population 2020, statistical release 1: Demographic characteristics, education, language and religion*. www.singstat.gov.sg/-/media/files/publications/cop2020/sr1/cop2020sr1.pdf

Development Bureau. (2016). *Hong Kong 2030+: Towards a planning vision and strategy transcending 2030*. www.hk2030plus.hk/document/2030+Booklet_Eng.pdf

Elder Academy. (2020). *About elder academy*. www.elderacademy.org.hk/en/aboutea/index.html

Fan, H. (2020). *Hospital authority welcomes policy address*. www.info.gov.hk/gia/general/202011/25/P2020112500749.htm

Feng, I., Chen, J. H., Zhu, B. W., & Xiong, L. (2018). Assessment of and improvement strategies for the housing of healthy elderly: Improving quality of life. *Sustainability*, *10*(3), 722. https://doi.org/10.3390/su10030722

Fonseca, L. M., Domingues, J. P., & Dima, A. M. (2020). Mapping the sustainable development goals relationships. *Sustainability*, *12*(8), 3359. https://doi.org/10.3390/su12083359

Ghaedrahmati, S., & Shahsavari, F. (2019). Affordable housing: elderly in Tehran and their housing problems. *Journal of Housing for the Elderly*, *33*(2), 140–152. https://doi.org/10.1080/02763893.2018.1534179

Gong, F., Zheng, Z. C., & Ng, E. (2016). Modeling elderly accessibility to urban green space in high density cities: A case study of Hong Kong. *Procedia Environmental Sciences*, *36*, 90–97. https://doi.org/10.1016/j.proenv.2016.09.018

The Government of the Hong Kong Special Administrative Region. (2016). *LCQ 13: Housing for elderly.* www.info.gov.hk/gia/general/201604/13/P201604130432. htm

The Government of the Hong Kong Special Administrative Region. (2019). *LCQ 8: The government's greening efforts.* www.info.gov.hk/gia/general/201905/15/P2019051500392.htm?fontSize=1

Han, K. M., Han, C., Shin, C., Jee, H. J., An, H., Yoon, H. K., . . . & Kim, S. H. (2018). Social capital, socioeconomic status, and depression in community-living elderly. *Journal of Psychiatric Research, 98,* 133–140. https://doi.org/10.1016/j.jpsychires.2018.01.002

Hirai, H., Kondo, K., & Kawachi, I. (2012). Social determinants of active aging: Differences in mortality and the loss of healthy life between different income levels among older Japanese in the AGES cohort study. *Current Gerontology and Geriatrics Research, 2012.* 701583. https://doi.org/10.1155/2012/701583

Hong Kong Housing Authority. (2019). *Senior citizens.* www.housingauthority.gov.hk/en/public-housing/meeting-special-needs/senior-citizens/index.html

Hong Kong Housing Society. (2021a). *Rent assistance scheme.* www.housingauthority.gov.hk/en/public-housing/rent-related-matters/rent-assistance-scheme/index.html

Hong Kong Housing Society. (2021b). *Ageing-in-place scheme.* www.hkhs.com/en/our-business/elderly-housing/ageing-in-place

Hospital Authority. (2021). *Waiving of medical charges (For eligible persons).* www.ha.org.hk/visitor/ha_visitor_index.asp?Parent_ID=10047&Content_ID=259365&Ver=HTML

Hui, E. C., Wong, F. K., Chung, K. W., & Lau, K. Y. (2014). Housing affordability, preferences and expectations of elderly with government intervention. *Habitat International, 43,* 11–21. https://doi.org/10.1016/j.habitatint.2014.01.010

Information Services Department. (2018, November 2). *Making a better HK for seniors.* www.news.gov.hk/eng/2018/11/20181102/20181102_150613_839.html

Jarzebski, M. P., Elmqvist, T., Gasparatos, A., Fukushi, K., Eckersten, S., Haase, D., . . . Pu, J. (2021). Ageing and population shrinking: Implications for sustainability in the urban century. *NPJ Urban Sustainability, 1*(1), 1–11. https://doi.org/10.1038/s42949-021-00023-z

Jayantha, W. M., & Abeydeera, L. H. U. W. (2019). Housing consumption of the "Soon-to-Retire" in Hong Kong: A cross-sectional regression analysis. *Asian Journal of Economics and Empirical Research, 6*(1), 76–84. https://doi.org/10.20448/journal.501.2019.61.76.84

Kim, G. M., Hong, M. S., & Noh, W. (2018). Factors affecting the health-related quality of life in community-dwelling elderly people. *Public Health Nursing, 35*(6), 482–489. https://doi.org/10.1111/phn.12530

Kim, J. I., & Kim, G. (2016). Relationship between the remaining years of healthy life expectancy in older age and national income level, educational attainment, and improved water quality. *The International Journal of Aging and Human Development, 83*(4), 402–417. https://doi.org/10.1177%2F0091415016657560

Kyriopoulos, I. I., Zavras, D., Skroumpelos, A., Mylona, K., Athanasakis, K., & Kyriopoulos, J. (2014). Barriers in access to healthcare services for chronic patients in times of austerity: An empirical approach in Greece. *International Journal for Equity in Health, 13*(54), 1–7. https://doi.org/10.1186/1475-9276-13-54

Labour and Welfare Bureau. (2021). *Government public transport fare concession scheme for the elderly and eligible persons with disabilities (the $2 scheme).* www.lwb.gov.hk/en/highlights/fare_concession/index.html

Lam, C. Y. H., & Fong, B. Y. F. (2020). "Ageing in place": Social and health implications in Hong Kong. *CAHMR Working Paper, 1*(1), 1–10. http://weblib.cpce-polyu.edu.hk/apps/wps/assets/pdf/cw20200101.pdf

Lam, C. Y. H., Lee, J. W. Y., & Chan, T. C. (2021). Town planning and community development: Healthy and happy housing. In B. Y. F. Fong & M. C. S. Wong. (Eds.), *The Routledge handbook of public health and the community.* Routledge, Singapore.

Lau, K. K. L., Yung, C. C. Y., & Tan, Z. (2021). Usage and perception of urban green space of older adults in the high-density city of Hong Kong. *Urban Forestry & Urban Greening, 64,* 127251. https://doi.org/10.1016/j.ufug.2021.127251

Leisure and Cultural Services Department. (2021). *Statistics report.* www.lcsd.gov.hk/en/aboutlcsd/ppr/statistics/leisure.html#act

Leung, D. S., & Liu, B. C. (2011). Lifelong education, quality of life and self-efficacy of Chinese older adults. *Educational Gerontology, 37*(11), 967–981. https://doi.org/10.1080/03601277.2010.492732

Leung, M., Yu, J., & Chow, H. (2016). Impact of indoor facilities management on the quality of life of the elderly in public housing. *Facilities, 34*(9/10), 564–579. https://doi.org/10.1108/f-06-2015-0044

Lewis, B., Purser, K., & Mackie, K. (2020). *The human rights of older persons.* Springer, Singapore. https://doi.org/10.1007/978-981-15-6735-3

Liu, P., & Lam, J. (2018, August 20). Nearly half of Hong Kong flats rent for US$2,550 a month – 70 per cent of median household income. *South China Morning Post.* www.scmp.com/business/article/2160554/nearly-half-hk-flats-rent-us2550-month-70-cent-median-household-income

Ma, X., & McGhee, S. M. (2013). A cross-sectional study on socioeconomic status and health-related quality of life among elderly Chinese. *BMJ Open, 3*(2), e002418. http://doi.org/10.1136/bmjopen-2012-002418

Mestheneos, E., & Withnall, A. (2016). Ageing, learning and health: Making connections. *International Journal of Lifelong Education, 35*(5), 522–536. https://doi.org/10.1080/02601370.2016.1224039

Muka, T., Imo, D., Jaspers, L., Colpani, V., Chaker, L., van der Lee, S. J., . . . Franco, O. H. (2015). The global impact of non-communicable diseases on health-care spending and national income: A systematic review. *European Journal of Epidemiology, 30*(4), 251–277. https://doi.org/10.1007/s10654-014-9984-2

Ng, A. (2019). Mental health impacts on people living in subdivided flats in Hong Kong. *Prehospital and Disaster Medicine, 34*(1), S150. https://doi.org/10.1017/S1049023X19003352

Ng, A. W., Ben, Y. F., & Leung, T. C. H. (2018a). Health and sustainability: Reinforcing public and private engagement through tertiary institutions. In U. Azeiterio, M. L. Akerman, L. W. Filho, A. Setti, & L. Brandli (Eds.), *Lifelong learning and education in healthy and sustainable cities* (pp. 169–186). World

Sustainability Series, Springer International Publishing, Switzerland. https://doi.org/10.1007/978-3-319-69474-0_10

Ng, A. W., Leung, T. C. H., & Ho, J. C. K. (2018b). Development of accreditation approach of elderly care service providers: Experience from East and West. In P. Yuen, A. W. Ng, & B. Fong (Eds.), *Sustainable health and long-term care solutions for an aging population* (pp. 126–144). IGI Global, Pennsylvania. https://doi.org/10.4018/978-1-5225-2633-9.ch007

Nugent, R., Bertram, M. Y., Jan, S., Niessen, L. W., Sassi, F., Jamison, D. T., . . . Beaglehole, R. (2018). Investing in non-communicable disease prevention and management to advance the sustainable development goals. *The Lancet*, *391*(10134), 2029–2035. https://doi.org 10.1016/s0140–6736(18)30667–6

Patil, D. S., Yadav, U. N., George, S., Helbich, M., Ettema, D., & Bailey, A. (2020). Developing an evidence-informed framework for safe and accessible urban mobility infrastructures for older adults in low-and middle-income countries: A protocol for realist synthesis. *Systematic Reviews*, *9*(1), 1–6. https://doi.org/10.1186/s13643-020-01456-w

Planning Department. (2016). *2030 transport infrastructure and traffic review*. www.hk2030plus.hk/document/Transport%20Infrastructure%20and%20Traffic%20Review_Eng.pdf

Ramirez-Rubio, O., Daher, C., Fanjul, G., Gascon, M., Mueller, N., Pajín, L., . . . Nieuwenhuijsen, M. J. (2019). Urban health: An example of a "health in all policies" approach in the context of SDGs implementation. *Globalization and Health*, *15*(1), 1–21. https://doi.org/10.1186/s12992-019-0529-z

Research Office. (2021). *Welfare services*. www.legco.gov.hk/research-publications/english/2021issh30-public-transport-fare-concession-20210625-e.pdf

Schneider-Skalska, G. (2019). Healthy housing environment in sustainable design. *IOP Conference Series: Materials Science and Engineering, 471*, 1–10. https://doi.org/10.1088/1757-899X/471/9/09208

Social Welfare Department. (2021). *Social Security Allowance (SSA) scheme*. www.swd.gov.hk/en/index/site_pubsvc/page_socsecu/sub_ssallowance/index.html

Solomon, E. M., Wing, H., Steiner, J. F., & Gottlieb, L. M. (2020). Impact of transportation interventions on health care outcomes: A systematic review. *Medical Care, 58*(4), 384–391. https://doi.org/10.1097/MLR.0000000000001292

Srichuae, S., Nitivattananon, V., & Perera, R. (2016). Aging society in Bangkok and the factors affecting mobility of elderly in urban public spaces and transportation facilities. *IATSS Research, 40*(1), 26–34. https://doi.org/10.1016/j.iatssr.2015.12.004

Stolz, E., Mayerl, H., Waxenegger, A., & Freidl, W. (2017). Explaining the impact of poverty on old-age frailty in Europe: Material, psychosocial and behavioural factors. *The European Journal of Public Health, 27*(6), 1003–1009. https://doi.org/10.1093/eurpub/ckx079

Tam, M. (2016). Later life learning experiences: Listening to the voices of Chinese elders in Hong Kong. *International Journal of Lifelong Education, 35*(5), 569–585. https://doi.org/10.1080/02601370.2016.1224042

Tam, M. (2018). Lifelong learning for older adults: Culture and Confucianism. In M. Milana, S. Webb, J. Holford, R. Waller, & P. Jarvis (Eds.), *The Palgrave international handbook on adult and lifelong education and learning* (pp. 857–878). Palgrave Macmillan, London. https://doi.org/10.1057/978-1-137-55783-4_44

Tam, M. (2019). Third age learning in Hong Kong: The elder academy experience. In M. Formosa (Ed.), *The university of the third age and active ageing: International perspectives on aging* (pp. 169–180). Springer, Cham. https://doi.org/10.1007/978-3-030-21515-6_14

Tam, M., & Chui, E. (2015). Ageing and learning: What do they mean to elders themselves? *Studies in Continuing Education, 38*(2), 195–212. https://doi.org/10.1080/0158037X.2015.1061492

Transport Department. (2021). *Smart device for the elderly and the disabled.* www.td.gov.hk/en/transport_in_hong_kong/pedestrians/pedestrian_crossing_facilities/smart_device/index.html

United Nations. (2016). *Report of the inter-agency and expert group on sustainable development goal indicators.* https://unstats.un.org/unsd/statcom/47th-session/documents/2016-2-IAEG-SDGs-Rev1-E.pdf

Urban Reform Institute. (2021). *Demographia international housing affordability 2021 edition.* www.demographia.com/dhi.pdf

Urban Renewal Authority. (2021). *Redevelopment.* www.ura.org.hk/en/redevelopment

Wagstaff, A. (2002). Poverty and health sector inequalities. *Bulletin of the World Health Organization, 80*(2), 97–105.

Wang, D., Lau, K. K. L., Yu, R., Wong, S. Y., Kwok, T. T., & Woo, J. (2017). Neighbouring green space and mortality in community-dwelling elderly Hong Kong Chinese: A cohort study. *BMJ Open, 7*(7), e015794. https://doi.org/10.1136/bmjopen-2016-015794

Widener, M. J., & Hatzopoulou, M. (2016). Contextualizing research on transportation and health: a systems perspective. *Journal of Transport & Health, 3*(3), 232–239. https://doi.org/10.1016/j.jth.2016.01.008

Wong, M., Yu, R., & Woo, J. (2017a). Effects of perceived neighbourhood environments on self-rated health among community-dwelling older Chinese. *International Journal of Environmental Research and Public Health, 14*(6), 614. https://doi.org/10.3390/ijerph14060614

Wong, R. C. P., Szeto, W. Y., Yang, L., Li, Y. C., & Wong, S. C. (2017b). Elderly users' level of satisfaction with public transport services in a high-density and transit-oriented city. *Journal of Transport & Health, 7*, 209–217. https://doi.org/10.1016/j.jth.2017.10.004

Woo, J., Yu, R., Cheung, K., & Lai, E. T. C. (2020). How much money is enough? Poverty and health in older people. *The Journal of Nutrition, Health & Aging, 24*(10), 1111–1115. https://doi.org/10.1007/s12603-020-1444-y

World Health Organization. (2018). *WHO housing and health guidelines: Executive summary.* https://apps.who.int/iris/handle/10665/277465

Wu, C., Smit, E., Xue, Q. L., & Odden, M. C. (2018). Prevalence and correlates of frailty among community-dwelling Chinese older adults: The China health and retirement longitudinal study. *The Journals of Gerontology: Series A, 73*(1), 102–108. https://doi.org/10.1093/gerona/glx098

Wu, X., & Wang, Z. (2019). Role of socioeconomic status in hypertension among Chinese middle-aged and elderly individuals. *International Journal of Hypertension, 2019.* https://doi.org/10.1155/2019/6956023

Wu, Y. T., Daskalopoulou, C., Muniz Terrera, G., Sanchez Niubo, A., Rodríguez-Artalejo, F., Ayuso-Mateos, J. L., Bobak, M., . . . Prina, A. M. (2020). Education and wealth inequalities in healthy ageing in eight harmonised cohorts in the ATHLOS consortium: A population-based study. *The Lancet Public Health, 5*(7), e386–e394. https://doi.org/10.1016/S2468-2667(20)30077-3

Yee, H. H. L., Fong, B. Y. F., Ng, T. K. C., & Law, V. T. S. (2021). Healthy ageing and lifelong learning: A case of senior citizens in Hong Kong. In B. Y. F. Fong & V. T. S. Law (Eds.), *Ageing with dignity in Asia: Holistic and humanistic care.* Springer, Singapore.

Yogo, M. (2016). Portfolio choice in retirement: Health risk and the demand for annuities, housing, and risky assets. *Journal of Monetary Economics, 80,* 17–34. https://doi.org/10.1016/j.jmoneco.2016.04.008

Yu, A. (2021). Open space and sense of community of older adults: A study in a residential area in Hong Kong. *International Journal of Architectural Research.* https://doi.org/10.1108/ARCH-11-2020-0260

Yu, R., Wang, D., Leung, J., Lau, K., Kwok, T., & Woo, J. (2018). Is neighborhood green space associated with less frailty? Evidence from the Mr. and Ms. Os (Hong Kong) study. *Journal of the American Medical Directors Association, 19*(6), 528–534. https://doi.org/10.1016/j.jamda.2017.12.015

Yuen, S. W. (2016). *Public transport policy measures to improve the mobility of the elderly in Hong Kong.* www.pico.gov.hk/doc/en/research_report(PDF)/2014_A8_025_15B_Final_Report_Dr_Szeto.pdf

Yung, E. H. K., Conejos, S., & Chan, E. H. W. (2016a). Social needs of the elderly and active aging in public open spaces in urban renewal. *Cities, 52,* 114–122. https://doi.org/10.1016/j.cities.2015.11.022

Yung, E. H. K., Conejos, S., & Chan, E. H. W. (2016b). Public open spaces planning for the elderly: The case of dense urban renewal districts in Hong Kong. *Elsevier, 59,* 1–11. https://doi.org/10.1016/j.landusepol.2016.08.022

4 Effectiveness of policy and services in elderly care in Hong Kong

This chapter will evaluate the effectiveness of the policy and services on the delivery of elderly care in response to the ageing population in Hong Kong, drawing on available literature and government publication as concluding remarks of SDG 3 and ageing. Policy recommendations for promoting healthy ageing and well-being for the elderly in Hong Kong would be proposed.

Being a global initiative, the SDGs have an enormous potential to transform people's health in the social, economic and environmental aspects (Bjegovic-Mikanovic et al., 2019). SDGs are comprehensive and universal initiatives that require countries or regions to achieve set targets and ensure that no one is left behind (Kamau & MacNaughton, 2019). From an environmental perspective, the SDGs foster people to adopt a healthier lifestyle while their environments are also improved (Bjegovic-Mikanovic et al., 2019). To achieve SDGs, concerted efforts of all economies are needed, so Hong Kong is not alone. Hence the various sectors of Hong Kong, including the public, private and third sectors should cooperate in social, economic, political, legal and environmental realms.

Substantial transformation is needed while health promotion plays a crucial role (Morita et al., 2020). Since the SDGs are broad in nature and there are limited specific instructions on implementation, policymakers can borrow and adapt SDGs as appropriate in their own contexts (Kamau & MacNaughton, 2019). While the implementation of the SDGs is an opportunity for many countries or regions in various aspects, it also poses considerable challenges. Attaining sustainable change through multisectoral action can be difficult to demonstrate or even to implement (Monteiro, 2020). Since the interlinkage among goals and individual SDGs are inseparably linked by an input-output correlation, their implementation needs systemic thinking (Breuer et al., 2019). Overall speaking, population health gains the greatest benefits from sustainable growth and is pivotal to achieving the SDGs (Haywood & Wright, 2019). For the benefits of Hong Kong citizens and public health, Hong Kong should

DOI: 10.4324/9781003220169-4

devise public policy in various realms, including food and health realms, to endeavour the achievement of the SDG 3, which ultimately benefit the city to achieve other SDGs as well.

Effectiveness of policy and services in elderly care in Hong Kong

Among the 13 targets under SDG 3, three of them are related to reproductive health and children's health; another three are related to communicable diseases, chronic diseases and addictive behaviours; two are related to environmental health; one is related to universal health coverage; and four are related to the use of tobacco, vaccines and medicines, and preparedness to address global health risks. Since SDG 3 is interconnected with other SDGs, achievement of SDG 3 targets is crucial to the achievement of other SDG targets (Guegan et al., 2018). For example, the achievement of SDG 3 through sustainable diets and physical activity would be indirectly linked to other SDGs (Macassa, 2021). One of the major challenges is to comply with the SDGs while the COVID-19 pandemic has been draining economic, political and technological resources (Khetrapal & Bhatia, 2020). Nevertheless, SDG 3 possesses some limitations for conducting policy formation, policy coherence and implementation of programmes to enhance performance of the national health systems (Seidman, 2017).

Achievement of SDG 3 requires various resources, while both the government and private sector can provide sufficient investment resources (Buse & Hawkes, 2015). While national or local primary healthcare organisational models and available resources vary, many of the sustainable development challenges assessed in SDG 3 can be realised through citizen-centred health policies and population-based approaches. The Food and Health Bureau has the mandate to devise people-centred policy to ensure healthy lives and advance well-being of Hong Kong citizens, particularly the elderly, with the support of both public and private resources.

From a socio-economic perspective, trust is a vital factor in achieving SDG 3 goals while trust is fostered on the evaluation of the effective use of limited resources (Asi & Williams, 2018). In terms of elderly care services in Hong Kong, Hong Kong should further improve the services by building trust among the government, the private sector, service providers of elderly care, the elderly and their caretakers. On one hand, academic research with proactive participation of the service providers is needed to evaluate the outcomes of resources deployed in elderly care. On the other hand, trust-building policy initiatives are needed for insufficient or mismanaged service areas in elderly care.

Policy recommendations for elderly care in Hong Kong

From the public policy perspective, implementation of the SDGs requires policy coherence and participation of various actors other than the government (Breuer et al., 2019). Policy implementation is a key and the most important measure in realising the SDGs (Cheng et al., 2021). In order to control the SDG 3, it is imperative that public policies should be evaluated to achieve the SDGs (da Silva et al., 2021). To achieve SDGs related to elderly care in Hong Kong, the government needs to be proactive in soliciting support of the private sector, the NGOs and the citizens in realising the following policy recommendations.

Proactive formulation of post-COVID-19 public policy for the elderly

There are few studies that take into account the effects of COVID-19 on the SDGs (Khetrapal & Bhatia, 2020). Mental health and well-being may be affected by social isolation measures during the COVID-19 pandemic (da Silva et al., 2021). Although the spreading of COVID-19 in the world is not contained yet, the Hong Kong government needs to be proactive in formulating public policy to prepare for the post-COVID-19 era. Christ and Burritt (2019) advocate that the achievement of universal health coverage can be achieved quickly and effectively if various countries share their experiences. The reasons for weak and unequal health would also be clarified upon experience sharing (Di Ruggiero, 2019). During the formulation process, the Hong Kong government should share information with other countries or regions, especially those in the Asia-Pacific Region, and learn from overseas experience.

Moreover, SDG 3 encourages a restructuring of the health system and, hence, reinforcing the migration to universal health coverage (Seidman, 2017). Moreover, policymakers should design the optimal mix of policy instruments to maximise effectiveness of policy (Pitelis et al., 2020) and reach an equilibrium state (Xie et al., 2021). In addition, the policymakers of Hong Kong should review and adjust its portfolio of policy instruments related to elderly care in Hong Kong. They should adopt an interdisciplinary approach that can promote public health through sustainable behaviours of the citizens (Macassa, 2021). Ultimately, healthy lifestyles of individuals and communities are the direct context of sustainable development (Macassa, 2021).

Enhanced private sector involvement via public-private partnerships

The World Economic Forum (2015) recognised that the private sector can contribute to realising SDG 3. SDGs allow the private businesses to participate in public health through various means; for example, activities related to value chains, communication, occupational health and employee assistances (Haywood & Wright, 2019). In many countries, achievement of SDG 3 targets can be realised via the mobilisation and allocation of local resources by the private sector (Bali & Taaffe, 2017), as well as providing financial mechanisms and expertise in developing human capital and research (De Wolf & Toebes, 2016). Besides, private business can provide innovative technologies for data collection, improve disease monitoring, as well as improve supply chain management for essential health supplies (Haywood & Wright, 2019).

One of the most recommended financing instruments to achieve the SDG 3 targets is public-private partnership (PPP) (Wang & Ma, 2020). PPP for public health can improve access to pharmaceuticals in developing countries upon the development of new technologies (Reich, 2000). Although PPP have been in place in Hong Kong for years, the Hong Kong government may further deploy various types of resources provided by the private business sector and health organisations via PPP programmes. PPP initiatives demand an open dialogue among various stakeholders, including health professionals in both the public and private sectors, non-government organisations, academics, community leaders and the government, who play the leading and coordinating roles. Once the programmes are implemented, regular reviews and continuous improvement will help to steer PPP in maximising the impacts to the community.

Enhanced deployment of gerontechnology in elderly care services

Application of technology can raise the efficiency and improve the effectiveness of elderly care services, whereas an active healthy life for the elderly is maintained. To achieve SDG 3 successfully, access to new technologies and health knowledge, as well as technological development of healthcare organisations are vital (Grynko et al., 2020).

Gerontechnology are innovations and technologies tailor-made to the personal needs of older persons to compensate for cognitive and physical decline due to ageing (Beard et al., 2011). Gerontechnology helps older persons to age comfortably on a self-reliant basis (Beard et al., 2011). Gerontechnology is one of the major age-enablers, which is potentially beneficial to the elderly and relieves pressure on public health resources (OHKF, 2017). Gerontechnology can serve three functions: (a) assist the elderly to improve the quality of life, for example, remote monitoring devices at home or portable sensor-based alarm systems; (b) enhance physical functions of the elderly, for example, computerised therapeutic training devices or robotic training devices; (c) improve communication of the elderly with family members and caretakers (Research Office of Legislative Council Secretariat, 2018).

Promotion of digital health and telemedicine

In 2017, a working group of the Elderly Commission of Hong Kong devised an "Elderly Services Programme Plan" (ESPP) and gave 20 recommendations to improve elderly services in Hong Kong (Elderly Commission, 2017). One of the recommendations is to further promote the use of information and communication technology (ICT) for the elderly, their family members, caregivers and services providers. It is recommended that there is more assessable information for optimising the utilisation of service, improving the quality of life for the elderly and delivering quality service by the service providers. Firstly, an integrated service provider interface with the long-term care services delivery system (LDS) should be built, while enhancing the Standardised Care Need Assessment Mechanism for Elderly Services (SCNAMES) functions. Secondly, it is recommended that resources should be allocated to further enhance the effective use of ICT to boost digital inclusion and empower better health management. Thirdly, the use of ICT should be enhanced to further improve service quality of health. To ensure healthy lives and promote well-being for all at all ages in Hong Kong, various stakeholders of elderly care in Hong Kong, which include policymakers, healthcare professionals, the private sector and NGOs should collaborate in tackling the gaps and obstacles faced by the gerontechnology industry in Hong Kong (OHKF, 2017).

Digital health can reduce the influence of geographic barriers (Smoyer et al., 2016). The proliferation of mobile phones can revolutionise healthcare delivery (Asi & Williams, 2018). Mobile phone technology can quantify and mitigate the spread of various contagious diseases such as malaria and Ebola (Larocca et al., 2016). Telemedicine can improve health literacy via remote training, online modules (Ratzan, 2011) and remote monitoring where labour safety is compromised or education is inadequate (Asi & Williams, 2018). People actively search and evaluate health-related information by various means (Mayer, 2017). To meet health-related development goals, one of the most significant ways is to promote health literacy (Asi & Williams, 2018). Health literacy can also reduce the spreading of non-communicable diseases (ECOSOC, 2010).

In the Hong Kong context, telemedicine has been tried by the public system years ago and is provided by a few private or non-governmental organisations. Although the spreading of COVID-19 in Hong Kong triggers a few small-scale telemedicine in the public sector, its coverage is still limited and does not substantially help warranting healthy lives and fostering well-being of citizens. It is recommended that as far as the legal stipulation on the provision of services is not violated, the government should consider further promoting telemedicine.

Strengthening of primary care workforce to relieve crises of doctor shortage

To achieve universal health coverage of the SDG 3, the healthcare system needs a reinforced health workforce and enhanced supply of health facilities, equipment, medicines and vaccines (World Health Organization, 2019). The government should also remove barriers to getting services, which include economic barriers due to out-of-pocket payments and inadequate public financing (World Health Organization, 2019). Health and well-being are irritated by the shortage of health practitioners and poor access to health (Asi & Williams, 2018).

To tackle the shortage of medical doctors in Hong Kong, Our Hong Kong Foundation (2021) proposes system-level changes to the mix and distribution of Hong Kong's health workforce, which include building up and strengthening primary care workforce and leveraging allied health professionals. The government should proactively and boldly leverage the capacity of non-locally trained doctor in the immediate term.

Holistic end-of-life care for the elderly

World Health Organization (2016, p. 5) defined palliative care as is an approach that enhances the quality of life of patients and their families who are encountering problems related to lethal illness. It is the ethical responsibility of health systems to alleviate pain and suffering of end-of-life care for individuals since end-of-life care is one of the critical elements of palliative care (World Health Organization, 2016, p. 89). To promote well-being of the elderly at their late stage of life, Hong Kong needs a holistic and more sustainable health system to provide improved and dignified end-of-life service for the citizens (OHKF, 2019). Firstly, public education and policy advocacy on end-of-life care are needed. Secondly, the scope and quality of service of end-of-life care need to be improved. Thirdly, dying at home or staying in the community until the end of their lives should be supported, partly to provide a choice for the persons at the end of life and partly to reduce the burden of the hospitals.

References

Asi, Y. M., & Williams, C. (2018). The role of digital health in making progress toward Sustainable Development Goal (SDG) 3 in conflict-affected populations. *International Journal of Medical Informatics*, *114*, 114–120. https://doi.org/10.1016/j.ijmedinf.2017.11.003

Bali, S., & Taaffe, J. (2017). The Sustainable Development Goals and the global health security agenda: Exploring synergies for a sustainable and resilient world. *Journal of Public Health Policy, 38*(2), 257–268. https://doi.org/10.1057/s41271-016-0058-4

Beard, J. R., Biggs, S., Bloom, D. E., Fried, L. P., Hogan, P., Kalache, A., & Olshansky, S. J. (2011). *Global population ageing: Peril or promise?* World Economic Forum. http://www3.weforum.org/docs/WEF_GAC_GlobalPopulationAgeing_Report_2012.pdf

Bjegovic-Mikanovic, V., Abousbie, Z., Breckenkamp, J., Wenzel, H., Broniatowski, R., Nelson, C., Vukovic, D., & Laaser, U. (2019). A gap analysis of SDG 3 and MDG 4/5mortality health targets in the six Arabic countries of North Africa: Egypt, Libya, Tunisia, Algeria, Morocco, and Mauritania. *The Libyan Journal of Medicine, 14*(1), 1607698. https://doi.org/10.1080/19932820.2019.1607698

Breuer, A., Janetschek, H., & Malerba, D. (2019). Translating Sustainable Development Goal (SDG) interdependencies into policy advice. *Sustainability, 11*, 2092.

Buse, K., & Hawkes, S. (2015). Health in the sustainable development goals: Ready for a paradigm shirt? *Globalization and Health, 11*(1), 13. https://doi.org/10.1186/s12992-015-0098-8

Cheng, Y., Liu, H., Wang, S., Cui, X., & Li, Q. (2021). Global action on SDGs: Policy review and outlook in a post-pandemic era. *Sustainability, 13*(11), 6461. https://doi.org/10.3390/su13116461

Christ, K. L., & Burritt, R. L. (2019). Implementation of sustainable development goals: The role for business academics. *Australian Journal of Management, 44*(4), 571–593. https://doi.org/10.1177%2F0312896219870575

da Silva, F. R., Câmara, S. F., Pinto, F. R., Soares, M., Viana, M. B., & de Paula, T. M. (2021). Sustainable development goals against Covid-19: The performance of Brazilian cities in SDGs 3 And 6 and their reflection on the pandemic. *Geography Environment Sustainability, 14*, 9–16. https://doi.org/10.24057/2071-9388-2020-188

De Wolf, A., & Toebes, B. (2016). Assessing private sector involvement in health care and universal health coverage in light of the right to health. *Health and Human Rights, 18*(2), 79–92.

Di Ruggiero, E. (2019). Health promotion in the sustainable development goal era. *Global Health Promotion, 26*(3), 3–4. https://doi.org/10.1177%2F17579759198 74708

Elderly Commission. (2017). *Elderly services programme plan.* www.elderly commission.gov.hk/en/download/library/ESPP_Final_Report_Eng.pdf

Grynko, T., Shevchenko, T., Pavlov, R., Shevchenko, V., & Pawliszczy, D. (2020). The impact of collaboration strategy in the field of innovation on the effectiveness of organizational structure of healthcare institutions. *Knowledge and Performance Management, 4*(1), 37–51. https://doi.org/10.21511/kpm.04(1).2020.04

Guegan, J.-F., Suzan, G., Kati-Coulibaly, S., Bonpamgue, D. N., & Moatti, J.-P. (2018). Sustainable development goal #3, "health and well-being", and the need for more integrative thinking. *Veterinaria Mexico OA, 5*(2). https://doi.org/10.21753/vmoa.5.2.443

Haywood, L. K., & Wright, C. Y. (2019). Private sector contribution to SDG 3: Health and Well-being–a South African case study. *South African Journal of Science*, *115*(9/10). https://doi.org/10.17159/sajs.2019/6452

Kamau, E., & MacNaughton, G. (2019). The impact of SDG 3 on health priorities in Kenya. *Journal of Developing Societies*, *35*(4), 458–480. https://doi.org/10.1177/0169796X19874609

Khetrapal, S., & Bhatia, R. (2020). Impact of COVID-19 pandemic on health system & sustainable development goal 3. *Indian Journal of Medical Research*, *151*(5), 395–399.

Larocca, A., Visconti, R., & Marconi, M. (2016). Malaria diagnosis and mapping with mHealth and Geographic Information Systems (GIS): Evidence from Uganda. *Malarial Journal*, *15*(520), 1–12. https://doi.org/10.1186/s12936-016-1546-5

Macassa, G. (2021). Can sustainable health behaviour contribute to ensure healthy lives and wellbeing for all at all ages (SDG 3)? A viewpoint. *Journal of Public Health Research*. 10.4081/jphr.2021.2051. Advance online publication. https://doi.org/10.4081/jphr.2021.2051

Mayer, A. K. (2017). Assessing health information literacy by a knowledge test. *European Journal of Public Health*, *27*(Suppl. 3), 26. http://dx.doi.org/10.1093/eurpub/ckx187.066

Monteiro, B. R. (2020). Monitoring and performance indicators in family health units and the objectives of Sustainable Development Goals (SDG 3) in health: A comparative analysis in Portugal in the 2013–2018 period. Indicadores de monitorização e desempenho nas unidades de saúde familiar e os Objetivos do Desenvolvimento Sustentável na saúde (ODS 3): uma análise comparada em Portugal no período de 2013–2018. *Ciencia & saude coletiva*, *25*(4), 1221–1232. https://doi.org/10.1590/1413-81232020254.31422019

Morita, K., Okitasari, M., & Masuda, H. (2020). Analysis of national and local governance systems to achieve the sustainable development goals: Case studies of Japan and Indonesia. *Sustainability Science*, *15*(1), 179e202. https://doi.org/10.1007/s11625-019-00739-z

Our Hong Kong Foundation (OHKF). (2017). *Gerontechnology landscape report*. www.ourhkfoundation.org.hk/sites/default/files/media/pdf/healthtech_eng_cover_ss.pdf

Our Hong Kong Foundation (OHKF). (2019). *Fostering medical-social collaboration in achieving quality end-of-life care (Executive summary)*. https://ourhkfoundation.org.hk/sites/default/files/media/pdf/20191216_Medical-SocialCollabEOL Care.pdf

Our Hong Kong Foundation (OHKF). (2021). *Fit to practise: Reviving the role of non-locally trained doctors to strengthen Hong Kong's doctor workforce today for a better tomorrow healthcare research report*. https://ourhkfoundation.org.hk/ebook/HC_NEW/Healthcare_Manpower_Report_20210624/Eng_FULL/mobile/index.html

Pitelis, A., Vasilakos, N., & Chalvatzis, K. (2020). Fostering innovation in renewable energy technologies: Choice of policy instruments and effectiveness. *Renewable Energy*, *151*, 1163e1172. https://doi.org/10.1016/j.renene.2019.11.100

Ratzan, S. C. (2011). Connecting the MDGs and NCDs with digital health. *Journal of Health Communication, 16*(7), 681–685. https://doi.org/10.1080/10810730.20 11.600623

Reich, M. R. (2000). Public-private partnerships for public health. *Nature Medicine, 6*(6), 617–620. https://doi.org/10.1038/76176

Research Office of Legislative Council Secretariat. (2018). *Information note policy measures to promote smart elderly care services in selected places IN07/17–18.* www.legco.gov.hk/research-publications/english/1718in07-policy-measures-to-promote-smart-elderly-care-services-in-selected-places-20180228-e.pdf

Seidman, G. (2017). Does SDG 3 have an adequate theory of change for improving health systems performance? *Journal of Global Health, 7*(1), 010302. https://doi.org/10.7189/jogh.07.010302

Smoyer, W. E., Embi, P. J., & Moffatt-Bruce, S. (2016). Creating local learning health systems: Think globally, act locally. *JAMA, 316*(23), 2481–2482. https://doi.org/10.1001/jama.2016.16459

United Nations Economic and Social Council (ECOSOC). (2010). Health literacy and the millennium development goals: United Nations Economic and Social Council (ECOSOC) regional meeting background paper (Abstracted). *Journal of Health Communication, 15*(supp. 2), 211–223. https://doi.org/10.1080/10810 730.2010.499996

Wang, N., & Ma, M. (2020). Public-private partnership as a tool for sustainable development: What literatures say? *Sustainable Development, 29*(3), 243–258. https://onlinelibrary.wiley.com/doi/epdf/10.1002/sd.2127

World Economic Forum. (2015). *How can business improve global health?* www.weforum.org/agenda/2015/09/how-can-business-improve-global-health/

World Health Organization. (2016). *Planning and implementing palliative care services: A guide for programme managers.* World Health Organization. https://apps.who.int/iris/handle/10665/250584

World Health Organization. (2019). *World health statistics overview 2019: Monitoring health for the SDGs, sustainable development goals.* World Health Organization (WHO/DAD/2019.1). Licence: CC BY-NC-SA 3.0 IGO.

Xie, H., Wen, J., & Choi, Y. (2021). How the SDGs are implemented in China: A comparative study based on the perspective of policy instruments. *Journal of Cleaner Production, 291*, 125937. https://doi.org/10.1016/j.jclepro.2021.125937

Index

For Product Safety Concerns and Information please contact our EU representative GPSR@taylorandfrancis.com Taylor & Francis Verlag GmbH, Kaufingerstraße 24, 80331 München, Germany

Batch number: 08153772

Printed by Printforce, the Netherlands